ARE YOU A LIBERAL? ARE YOU A CONSERVATIVE?

MICHAEL KRONENWETTER

Are You a Liberal? Are You a Conser- vative?

A GROLIER COMPANY

FRANKLIN WATTS
New York | London | Toronto | Sydney | 1984
AN IMPACT BOOK

Photographs courtesy of: New York Public Library Picture Collection:
pp. 10, 25, 30, 48; The Bettmann Archive: p. 41; UPI: pp. 67, 81, 86.

Library of Congress Cataloging in Publication Data

Kronenwetter, Michael.
Are you a liberal? Are you a conservative?

(An Impact book)
Bibliography: p.
Includes index.
Summary: Describes two dominant political terms, their
history, and what they mean today.
1. Political science—History—Juvenile literature.
2. Right and left (Political science)—History—Juvenile
literature. [1. Liberalism. 2. Conservatism.
3. Political science—History] I. Title.
JA83.K73   1984   320.5'09   83-27417
ISBN 0-531-04751-2

CONTENTS

con • ser • va • tive (kən sur′və tiv) *adj.* [ME. &
OFr. *conservatif* <LL. *conservativus*] 1. conserving or tending to conserve 2. tending to
preserve established traditions or instutitions
or to oppose any changes in these (*conservative* politics) 3. of or characteristic of a conservative —*n.* 1. a conservative person

lib • er • al (lib′ər əl, lib′ rəl) *adj.* [ME. <OFr.
<L. *liberalis* <*liber*, free <IE. **leudhero-*,
belonging to the people, free <base **leudh-*,
to grow up, rise, whence G. *leute*, people, OE.
leudan, to grow] 1. giving freely 2. not restric-
ted to the literal meaning (a *liberal* interpreta-
tion of the rules) 3. tolerant of different views,
not orthodox 4. favoring reform—*n.* 1. a liberal
person

INTRODUCTION

In the broadest terms, to be liberal is to want things to change, and to be conservative is to want them to remain the same.

To some extent, then, everyone is *both* liberal and conservative. We would all like to change some things for the better. At the same time, we all instinctively fear any sudden and drastic change in our lives that might affect us in unforeseen and even dangerous ways. At one time or another we would all like greater freedom from the restraints and obligations placed on us by society, the government, or our families. At the same time, we all have a need for the security offered by at least some of those very institutions.

These conflicting impulses exist, sometimes in uncomfortable balance, in each of us. As it is for us as individuals, so it is for societies at large. All societies have conservative elements within them, acting to preserve the institutions which those societies have developed. At the same time, all societies have liberal elements within them, working to change those institutions for the better, or even to eliminate them altogether.

This struggle is so central to political life in a democracy that the terms "liberal" and "conservative" have come to be used to describe the two main currents of thought which have dominated political debate in the western world ever since the monarchies of Europe began to be overthrown in the late eighteenth century.

Those terms have been used to describe a confusing range of people and programs over the years, and they are often used loosely and confusingly today. And yet, it's important for citizens of a democracy to understand those terms, and the currents of thought they represent, in order to be prepared to make informed political choices of their own. One way for you to come to that understanding is to consider where those currents of thought originated in the first place, and to chart the sometimes twisting courses they've taken as they've flowed into the political realities of today.

This book is designed to help you do just that.

1

THE AGE OF ENLIGHTENMENT AND THE BIRTH OF LIBERALISM

Both liberalism and conservatism, as we understand them today, were born in the events surrounding the bloody revolutions which took place in France and America in the eighteenth century. Modern political liberalism had its beginnings in the Age of Enlightenment, which provided the philosophical basis for those revolutions, while modern conservatism sprang from a response to them. In a deeper sense, though, both were products of the long centuries of feudalism in Europe.

For almost a thousand years, the continent of Europe was divided into many kingdoms, each ruled by a monarch. Each kingdom was, in turn, divided into many fiefdoms— smaller pieces of land held by nobles under the authority of the king. In return, the lords were expected to support the power of the king, to pay him taxes, and to raise armies to fight his wars.

The majority of the people, however, were neither kings nor nobles. They were peasants, or serfs, who lived on the land belonging to the nobles and worked that land for their lords. They had no choice in the matter. They were born on a given piece of land and tied to it, and to the noble who ruled it, until death. If a peasant ever left the land on which he was born for any extended time, it was only to serve as a soldier, fighting for the same lord whose land he worked. The entire system was hereditary. Kings, nobles, and peasants alike were born into a clearly defined class and could never escape from it.

This feudal system operated with the blessing of the Church, which was perhaps the single most important force in Europe. The clergy were everywhere. They were the most educated class, the guardians not only of men's souls, but also of their minds. Not only theology, but science and even the arts were carried out almost exclusively under the auspices of the Church of Rome. And beyond that, the Church was the cement which held the political structure of feudal Europe together. The kings of most countries were crowned by a member of the clergy, and they derived their ultimate authority and legitimacy from the blessing of the Church.

This close tie between the Church and the monarchs eventually gave rise to a concept known as the divine right of kings. This held that the Christian kings of Europe had been chosen by God to rule their kingdoms. A challenge to the power of the king was, in effect, a challenge to the will of God.

This interconnected system of political and spiritual authority made for extraordinary stability. There were famines and plagues and wars, and even revolutions of a kind. Kings were sometimes overthrown by their rivals, and the boundaries of kingdoms changed, but these upheavals never threatened the basic structure of society. That feudal structure was so firmly rooted in tradition and theology as to seem unshakable.

It was an essentially conservative age. A resistance to change was built into the system. What changes did take place to the social and political structures came about not through any rational plan, but through the gradual evolution of the institutions of the society. That evolution was often so slow that it passed virtually unnoticed by the people in whose society the changes were taking place.

The most important of these changes was the rise of a new social class, one which would eventually bring down the whole feudal structure. This was the middle class, so called because it was positioned between the peasants and the nobility. It grew up because of changes which took place in the economy of Europe. Trade between nations increased dramatically toward the end of the Middle Ages, as advances in the technology of shipbuilding made commerce between the nations of Europe and those of other continents more and more practical.

Goods from Asia were specially prized, and they had to be paid for. Until then, the economy of Europe had been almost exclusively agricultural, and commerce had been carried out mostly by barter, exchanging one good for another. But once other countries and peoples had to be traded with, a more convenient and interchangeable trading medium had to be found. This need gave rise to the widespread use of money, in the form of gold and silver coins, both as a means of exchange and as a measure of wealth.

The discovery of the Americas presented Europe with a rich source of those precious metals. As a result, goods flooded into Europe from the east, while gold and silver flooded in from the west. The object of the trading policies of the European nations came to be to maintain a favorable balance of trade, that is, to sell more goods abroad than they purchased from abroad. This would result in a surplus of money (gold and silver), which could then finance other activities of the government, most often wars. In order to achieve this favorable balance of trade, the nations put tariffs on goods from abroad and adopted other policies designed to discourage imports and encourage exports.

Since trade was vital to national defense, the monarchs attempted to keep control of it in their hands. They set up companies to handle the trade for them. These companies acted under the authority of the king, and were expected to operate in the king's (and the nation's) best interest. This system, in which national policy and international trade were closely allied if not identical, was called mercantilism, and to make mercantilism work, a new class of people was necessary. Artisans were needed to produce the goods to be traded with other nations, as well as to build the ships to carry them; skilled seamen were needed to sail these ships; merchants were needed to handle the buying and the selling of the goods; and bankers were needed to finance the operations.

Consequently, as the economy of Europe changed from being almost exclusively rural and agricultural to being largely urban and mercantile, the new middle class, most of whom lived in the cities, grew rapidly. And so did its political power. At first, that power was used on the side of the king, but the true allegiance of the middle class was not to the king but to profitable trade and commerce. This was something new in Europe, a large and growing class whose members did not feel allegiance to the class above it, nor to the system itself, but to their own interests and to money. Those allegiances would eventually bring it into conflict with the monarchial feudal system.

THE ENLIGHTENMENT AND
THE APPEAL TO REASON

By the seventeenth century, there was another force in motion which would prove equally destructive to feudalism. That force was the scientific and philosophical movement which came to be called the Enlightenment. To call it a movement, however, is not to imply that it was an organized effort by a single group to accomplish a common goal. Rather, the Enlightenment consisted of the individual efforts of many philosophers and scientists who, in the roughly two centuries from about 1600 to 1800, changed the way that people in the western world thought about reality, and about mankind.

Among them, the thinkers of the Enlightenment examined virtually every aspect of reality—the physical world, the people who lived in it, and the social order that governed them. They found new ways of understanding and explaining these realities, and new ideas about what might be done to change them for the better.

While the ideas of the many scientists and philosophers

of the Enlightenment varied widely and were often in conflict with each other, they had certain aspects in common. The most important of these was a refusal to rely on religious faith as the primary guide to understanding reality. Throughout the Middle Ages, faith had been the foundation on which the European's view of reality—both physical and social—was built. Things were the way they were because God had willed them to be that way. If you wished to understand how they came about, you had to rely on God's word, transmitted through the Church, for the explanation. In the feudal understanding, the earth was the center of the physical universe, the king was the head of the state, and the Church was the cement which held God, man, and the social order together. Any questions about these things ultimately had to be resolved by faith in God's design for the universe.

The thinkers of the Enlightenment effectively did away with the reliance on faith as the ultimate authority on questions of reality. They asked questions that had not been seriously asked in the western world for centuries. Some of these questions had been considered closed, already answered by an appeal to God's word as found in the Bible. Others were simply considered irrelevant by a society which believed that all the truly important questions had already been answered.

Questions asked by the thinkers of the Enlightenment ranged from the location of the earth in the universe, to the reason an apple falls from a tree, to the ways in which the great mass of humanity might be made happier. And when the philosophers of the Enlightenment asked these questions, they asked them not in a spirit of faith, but in a spirit of skepticism.

However, if faith was no longer a sufficient authority on which to base one's view of reality, what could be relied on instead? The answer given by the Enlightenment was human reason—the mind of man. Human intelligence would be brought to bear on the great questions of the

Enlightenment. They would be examined not in the glow of unquestioning faith, but in the harsh light of scientific curiosity.

This was not a new concept. The ancient philosophers had relied heavily on reason to solve the puzzles of the universe. And even in Christian Europe as early as the thirteenth century, the great Church philosopher Thomas Aquinas had tried to reconcile the claims of faith and reason. Early on he had argued that there was no conflict between true faith and true reason, because both came from God. This synthesis of faith and reason was, in fact, the accepted belief of the Church throughout the late Middle Ages. But, the Church insisted, when there *seemed* to be a conflict between them, faith had to be relied on as the ultimate guide to the truth.

The Enlightenment effectively turned this priority around. Although many of the philosophers and scientists of the time were men of great religious faith themselves, their work had the effect of supplanting faith with reason as the final authority on scientific and even social questions. Because of this, the period of European history from about 1600 to about 1800 is known not only as the age of Enlightenment, but also as the age of reason.

The most important figure of the early enlightenment was a scientist, the Englishman Sir Isaac Newton. In a few short years, his work on the laws of motion and gravity answered a wide range of questions which had remained unanswered for all the thousands of years before. His investigations were a stunning example of what human reason could accomplish, and gave a great spur to those who followed him.

While Newton and other scientists were busy expanding people's knowledge about the physical sciences, others were turning their attention to the study of man himself. One of the first figures of the Enlightenment to combine the study of science and the study of man was a Frenchman, René Descartes. He apparently received some kind of

The French philosopher René Descartes
was one of the first thinkers to relate
scientific principles to the study of man,
laying the foundation for the Enlightenment.

vision, or dream, which inspired him with the conviction that the way to the truth about humanity was to be found through the principles of mathematics.

Although a devout Catholic, he started his investigations from a position of absolute skepticism and doubt. He refused to accept faith as a basis for anything. Instead, he used doubt itself as the proof of even his own existence. He doubted, therefore he could think. If he could think, he must exist. He summed up this proof in the famous phrase "*Cogito ergo sum*"—"I think, therefore I am." Then, from this proof of his own existence, he went on to argue the existence of the physical world around him, and ultimately of God, the Creator.

The details of Descartes' philosophy aren't important here, but he is significant as a forerunner of much of the Enlightenment—and later liberal—thought which came after him. His skepticism set a standard for such thought, as did his attempt to apply the principles and methods of science (in his case, primarily of mathematics) to the study of man. For while Descartes was a mathematician, with an almost mystical devotion to the principles of that science, the truth he sought was not the truth about numbers but the truth about people. He believed that mathematics could help him understand people and their society, and could somehow point the way toward improving both, so that mankind could be made happier than they were. The last major published work of this renowned mathematician was not about mathematics at all, but about psychology.

This concentration on the study of man, and ultimately on finding ways to promote human well-being and happiness, forms a major link between the Enlightenment and modern liberal political thinking.

THE SOCIAL CONTRACT

The way society was organized and the way people were governed, were of vital importance to their well-being, of course. The feudal monarchies of Europe had survived for nearly a thousand years, but they would not survive the Enlightenment.

While the Enlightenment's undermining of faith as the supreme authority on scientific and social questions was a threat to the dominant position of the Church in European society, it was also a threat to the monarchs of the continent. They ruled, after all, by divine right, and divine right was established by faith. If faith was to be removed as the authority in such matters, by what right could monarchs continue to rule?

One answer to this dilemma was provided by an English philosopher named Thomas Hobbes. He derived a theory that governments ruled by authority of a kind of social contract between the people and the government. Some strong form of government was necessary, Hobbes argued, because individual human beings were selfish and predatory. Since the goods of the earth are limited, and since everyone wants a large portion of them, there is inevitably competition between people. Without the order and restraints imposed by the state, people would be in perpetual conflict with each other. Everyone would live with constant violence or, at the very least, the fear of violence. Under such conditions of anarchy, Hobbes wrote in a famous phrase, human life would be "solitary, poor, nasty, brutish and short."

Since every individual's right to the good things of life was equal to every other individual's right, there was no rational way to determine who should get what, or be allowed this or that privilege. Therefore, some sovereign power had to be given the authority to make such decisions and to impose order. For Hobbes, the best form such a government could take was monarchy.

Such monarchies had, in fact, been established, and while the people might disagree with an action of their monarch, they accepted his rule, however arbitrary it was, because it saved them from the anarchy and violence that would exist without it. This was an implied contract between the people and the sovereign. As in all contracts, each party to the social contract had obligations. For its part, the sovereign kept society from disintegrating into anarchy. For their part, the people surrendered to the sovereign their freedom to act as they wished and to make their own decisions. For the people then, it was a necessary bargain—they gave up their freedom in return for security.

Hobbes' theory was essentially a conservative one, both because it was designed to justify the social order as it was (monarchy), and because it held that when a conflict arose between the rights of individuals and the security of society, security was the more important concern. These two elements, a preference for things as they are and an overriding concern for the security of the state, are central to conservative political thought.

But despite his conservatism, Hobbes was also important to the development of liberal political thought. For one thing, he was a part of the movement away from faith and toward human reason. For another, he was an empiricist. That is, he believed that the worth of any idea had to be demonstrated through actual experience. The ultimate test of any idea to an empiricist is not how appealing it is in theory, but how well it works in the real world. If it works, it's good. If it doesn't work, it isn't. The application of empirical reasoning to political thought results in a philosophy of pragmatism and experiment rather than a rigid adherence to a particular set of ideas. Such pragmatism is a major element of liberal political thinking.

Even more important to the future of liberalism was Hobbes' contention that each individual had an equal right to life and liberty. Therefore, no particular person or class had a natural right to anything better than any other person or class. The only way for such inequities to be justified was if some people surrendered their natural rights in order to obtain security, which they did in Hobbes' version of the social contract.

The concept of the social contract did not originate with Hobbes, but he was the one who applied it to seventeenth-century Europe and thereby made it an important element of Enlightenment thought. In a somewhat different form, it would provide one of the foundation stones of liberal philosophy.

That form of the social contract was devised by another English philosopher, John Locke. Where Hobbes was fundamentally a conservative, Locke was liberal. Even more of an empiricist than Hobbes, Locke took up his belief in the rights to life and liberty, but he added to them another essential right—the right to property. This right, for Locke, was based largely on labor. A person, he felt, had a positive right to what had been earned through his or her labors.

Locke, like Hobbes, believed that the legitimate power of a state derived from a social contract, but he disagreed about why the contract was necessary. Where Hobbes argued that life without it would be "brutish and short" because men were essentially selfish and mean, Locke believed that men were essentially good and meant to be happy. They didn't need a social contract to keep themselves from violence and anarchy, as Hobbes believed, but only because individuals couldn't judge for themselves the boundaries between their legitimate rights and the rights of others. In order for things to run smoothly and fairly, some general authority was needed to make and enforce such judgments.

For centuries, philosophy had centered on theology, and science had centered on the external realities of the physical world. Now the centers had moved. God was still in His heaven, but the attention of Enlightenment philosophers like Locke had shifted from heaven to earth, and from God to man. As the poet Alexander Pope put it: "The proper study of Mankind is Man."

Nor was this study of man undertaken out of idle curiosity. For the philosophers of the Middle Ages, man had seemed to be a finished creature. He was born in original sin, but still savable by the Grace of God for an eternity of happiness in heaven. During his life on earth, however, he was strictly limited by his own poor nature and locked into a social order approved by God.

But for Locke and many other thinkers of the Enlightenment, neither man nor the society he lived in was ever finished. They could both be improved. Locke believed that what people thought, and consequently how they behaved, was the result of their particular environment and their individual experience within it. If in a state of nature they would be both happy and good, whereas in the real world they were mostly unhappy and immoral, the fault must be in their experience in that world. Somehow that experience was twisting and perverting their basic natures.

According to Locke, that experience came in two kinds: the personal experience of each individual (his upbringings and education) and the general experience of the society in which he lived. Both kinds of experience helped to shape him, to make him good or bad, happy or unhappy. If they could be changed for the better, then man himself could be changed for the better. It was a staggering thought.

This idea—the idea that man was capable of improvement, even perfection—was an essentially liberal one, and one of the main legacies of the Enlightenment to the modern age. It would contribute much to the age of upheaval and revolution which followed, and would dominate much of the political discussion of the next three centuries.

THE SEED OF DEMOCRACY

Buried in Locke's philosophy (and even to some extent in Hobbes') was the seed of modern democracy. If all people were essentially equal, if they all had the same natural rights, then shouldn't they all have an equal say in how they should be governed? True, they could surrender some of those rights, or even all of them, by agreeing to the social contract—but what if they became unhappy with that social contract? Did they not have a right to break it?

Hobbes would say no. Locke said yes. Much more than Hobbes, he emphasized the duty of the sovereign under the social contract to protect the rights of the people. While Hobbes felt that the power granted to the sovereign should be absolute, Locke felt that it should be both limited and conditional. He went even further, arguing that in cases where the sovereign was a tyrant or the state made "illegal attempts upon . . . the Liberties and Properties" of its people, the people had a right to throw out the social contract altogether. They had a right to revolution. In some cases, when the sovereign had broken that contract by abusing rather than protecting his people, those people might have a positive obligation to revolt.

Others went even further than Locke. The English poet John Milton, for example, argued that the people had a right to overthrow their government anytime they wanted, simply because they wanted a different one. It didn't matter whether the original government was good or bad. The people, he believed, should be able to rewrite the social contract at will, whether the state had lived up to its obligations under that contract or not.

In either case, whether the state or the people broke the contract first, once it was broken the result would be upheaval. In a world emerging from feudalism—a world in which some people upheld the idea of a social contract while others argued the divine right of kings—the seed of democracy was also the seed of revolution.

That seed bore two great fruits late in the eighteenth century—the French and American revolutions. These two children of the Enlightenment were like two twins, the one handsome and well thought of, the other scarred and notorious, which sprang from the same womb but which led very different lives. Between them, they signaled the beginning of the end for the monarchies of Europe, and the adoption of democratic forms of government throughout the western world.

The American Revolution was the logical culmination of much of Enlightenment political and social theory. And like that theory, it was liberal in its ideals but essentially conservative in spirit. The French Revolution, on the other hand, carried the liberal ideals of the Enlightenment into a frenzy of radicalism. The excesses of the revolution in France discredited many of those liberal ideals in the minds of many in Europe and elsewhere, and a revulsion against those excesses helped to form the basis for the development of modern-day conservatism.

2

THE FRENCH REVOLUTION AND THE BIRTH OF CONSERVATISM

By the late eighteenth century, France was the most important country on the continent. Its culture, it's fashions, and even its language dominated the courts of Europe. By that time, too, the center of the Enlightenment had shifted across the Channel from England to France. The writer and philosopher Voltaire stood alone for his wit and style. Denis Diderot and Jean d'Alembert had produced their monumental *Encyclopédie*, a twenty-eight-volume collection of essays and pictures dealing with every subject imaginable, written by the leading men of letters of the time. It was a kind of summation of the Enlightenment, designed to change the way people thought.

But, while monarchs and nobles all over the European continent copied French customs, read French books, and spoke the French language, the monarch and nobles of France itself were on the verge of a final disaster. Despite the brilliance of French thought, despite the dazzle of the court at Versailles, France was about to explode into revolution.

Its economy was in a shambles, thanks partly to poor financial management, and partly to its having overextended itself in several wars. The government desperately needed to raise revenues, but the nobles and the clergy refused to be taxed. Having nowhere else to turn, King Louis XVI was forced to impose heavy, even crushing, taxes on the French middle class, the bourgeoisie. As a result, the bourgeoisie came to resent not only the classes above them, who refused to pay their fair share, but also the king himself.

THE SPIRIT OF
JEAN JACQUES ROUSSEAU

The disenchantment of the bourgeoisie was encouraged by many French writers of the time, who pointed out and railed against the injustices being worked on them. Chief among these social critics was Jean Jacques Rousseau. A literary giant in a country which took literature seriously, Rousseau was so enormously popular that it would be hard to overestimate his influence.

Like Locke, he believed that man was a product of his environment and his training. Naturally happy, he was made unhappy by his social arrangements. Although there was no going back to the times of "natural" innocence, it was possible, by changing society, to make mankind "happy." Happiness for Rousseau meant freedom; and freedom meant living under freely chosen restraints, dictated by reason and accepted because they were ultimately in the individual's own best interests.

Rousseau had his own version of the social contract. He held that there was a "general will" among the people which had to be obeyed, both by the government and by the individuals in a society. This "general will" was what made a government legitimate. Authority rested with the people. The people might delegate authority to a government, but they could not surrender it. If a government was contrary to the will of the people, they should no longer tolerate it.

Even more than their substance, the spirit of Rousseau's writings inspired the generation of revolution in France. Robespierre, one of the most extreme leaders of the French Revolution, said he slept with a copy of Rousseau by his bedside. Although what he had to say was not drastically different from what was said by other writers of the time, Rousseau spoke with a new passion. He had a gift for the ringing phrase. "Man is born free," he wrote, "and everywhere he is in chains!" This was not the logical formulation of a Hobbes or a Locke. This was a battle cry. Rousseau died in 1778, more than a decade before revolution broke out in France. But if any man who did not himself take part in it can be said to have been responsible for the French Revolution, that man was Jean Jacques Rousseau.

REVOLUTION

Largely untouched by the writings of Rousseau, since they couldn't read, were the great mass of the people of France. Most were peasants; some were still held in the bonds of actual serfdom. Virtually all of them were poor, with no stake at all in the social, economic, or political systems of France. Like the bourgeoisie, they were becoming increasingly alienated from the crown, and from the upper classes, who continued to cling to their privileges as the country collapsed around them.

As the economy grew steadily worse in the 1780s, growth in population outstripped growth in agricultural production. An unusually bad harvest in 1788 brought hunger to thousands, perhaps even hundreds of thousands, of Frenchmen. Food prices soared. There were riots demanding food.

Desperately, Louis XVI called a meeting of the Estates-General. This was a body made up of representatives of the three most powerful classes in France: the nobility, the clergy, and what were called the "commons" or "towns," the bourgeoisie. The king hoped that the three classes might be able to work together to find some system of reforms and compromises which would hold France together.

At the meeting of the Estates-General, the nobility sat on the king's right, while the bourgeoisie sat to his left. The nobility argued in favor of the status quo, of maintaining the social and political system as it was. The bourgeoisie argued in favor of reform, of removing some of the privileges of the upper classes. Because of the seating arrangements at the meetings, the conservative nobility came to be referred to as "the right," while the liberal bourgeoisie came to be referred to as "the left." (Those who pushed for compromise between them were called "the center.") Eventually, the same terms came to be applied to the political positions of the two groups—conservative positions being called "rightist" positions, and liberal positions being called "leftist." This terminology is still widely used today.

It did not take long for the bourgeoisie to see that the nobility and the clergy were not willing to surrender their privileges. Consequently, the bourgeoisie split off from the rest of the Estates-General and declared themselves to be a National Assembly. Their position was based on a democratic ideal—they were the people, they would rule.

Louis was forced to accept the existence of the National Assembly, but he sent troops to intimidate it. This and other actions provoked many residents of Paris, and they took to the streets, storming the hated prison known as the Bastille and freeing the political prisoners there. Although more power was then given to the National Assembly and order was restored in France, the spirit of revolution had been let loose, and it would be many years before it was chained again.

The National Assembly drew up a constitution which made France into a constitutional monarchy and brought sweeping reforms to virtually every aspect of French life. Elected judges replaced the old appointed ones. Where earlier all of France had been administered from the royal court at Versailles, now power was shared by elected local governments around the country. What political power remained centralized was taken out of the hands of the nobility and the clergy and placed in the hands of the National Assembly. Although the Catholic Church was maintained as a kind of state religion, its enormous properties were sold to help pay off the nation's huge foreign debt.

Although the National Assembly seemed to be accomplishing a great deal, discontent was growing in the country. Nobles and clergy who had been stripped of many of their privileges were angry. A number of devout Catholics of all classes were upset with the revolution's treatment of their Church. And even within the revolution itself, many Frenchmen were enraged by the continuation of even a constitutional monarchy. In August of 1789, a mob seized Louis and his family and virtually imprisoned them in the Tuilleries Palace in Paris. The monarchy was ended, and in January 1793, the king, along with his family, was eventually executed.

ACCOMPLISHMENTS
OF THE REVOLUTION

The French Revolution was the first revolution on the continent of Europe to be based on liberal ideals. Those ideals were summed up in one of the most important documents in history, the Declaration of the Rights of Man and of the Citizen, which was passed by the National Assembly in August of 1789. Based on the ideals of the spiritual father of the Revolution, Jean Jacques Rousseau, the Declaration is considered by many to be the noblest statement of the rights of citizens of a free country ever written.

It began by announcing that the rights of man were "natural" and "unalienable"—that is, that they were not privi-

*An artist's romanticized view
of Louis XVI surrounded
by an angry mob at the
Tuilleries Palace in Paris*

24

leges granted by the government, which the government could later take away at will. They were intrinsic.

"Men," the Declaration proclaimed, "are born and remain free and equal in rights." The freedom and equality of man were, of course, basic liberal principles of the Enlightenment. They didn't require that all social distinctions be abolished in the new French Republic which the National Assembly was setting up, but that henceforth such distinctions had to be based not on birth but on the "general good."

Chief among the "rights" asserted by the Declaration were the rights of "liberty, property, security and resistance to oppression." Freedom of speech and religion were also upheld, subject only to the greater right of security, or, put another way, of "public order."

Hundreds of thousands of copies of the Declaration were sent throughout France, so that the people could see, spelled out in language everyone could understand, exactly what the revolution was working for. Its effect was extraordinary. It has stood ever since as a standard for citizens to measure their governments against. Together with the American Declaration of Independence (which had been signed thirteen years earlier, and which clearly influenced it) and with the Constitution of the United States, the Declaration of the Rights of Man has formed the basis for scores of later national constitutions.

Another of the great accomplishments of the French Revolution was the abolition of slavery in the French colonies, an action clearly proceeding from the liberal beliefs in the freedom and equality of man. France was the first major country in the western world to take such action. (Britain, for example, didn't abolish slavery in its colonies until 1833, while the United States had internal slavery until after the Civil War.)

At home, the Revolution abolished feudalism in France itself. In August of 1789 (the same month in which the king was imprisoned and the Declaration of the Rights of Man was passed), the nobles and clergy bowed to the bourgeoisie and surrendered their privileges. Virtually the whole apparatus by which the aristocracy had exercised and maintained its power was dismantled in a single day. The social structure of France, which had survived for centuries upon centuries, had been overturned forever.

MASSACRES AND TERROR

The great liberal achievements of the Revolution—the Declaration of the Rights of Man, the abolishment of feudalism at home and slavery abroad—were purchased at an enormous cost. Those achievements came early, and they were followed by a decade of chaos, repression, and bloodshed which appalled moderate and conservative observers all over Europe.

The economic problems, which had been one of the main causes of the Revolution in the first place, quickly got worse instead of better. The necessity of fighting off the armies of other European powers hostile to the Revolution caused French government expenses to triple. Inflation soared, and the French currency lost ninety-five percent of its value within a few years.

The economic chaos was accompanied by social chaos. As the aristocracy of Europe looked on in horror, mobs seemed to take control of France. Starting with the storming of the Bastille, at turning point after turning point of the Revolution, mobs stormed through the streets of Paris. In the view of the foreign aristocracy, these mobs were made up of scum, people who, elsewhere in Europe, would have no say in events whatsoever. In revolutionary France, they were in control.

In August of 1792, mass arrests began in Paris. Some four thousand people—many of them priests and aristocrats, but large numbers of them members of the bourgeoisie— were thrown into prison. Then, in the first week of September, mobs of men entered the prisons and murdered some fifteen hundred prisoners. To many observers elsewhere in Europe, the September Massacres (as the murders were called) were further proof of the breakdown of sanity in France. But they were only a small taste of what was to come.

On January 21, 1793, King Louis XVI of France was executed, by guillotine. The event was profoundly shocking, not only to the aristocracy of the rest of Europe, but even within revolutionary France itself. It has been estimated that a substantial majority of the "free and equal" citizens of France were opposed to the execution of the king. Regicide, the murder of a monarch, was an act of particular horror for those raised in an age which had believed in the divine right of kings. Then, within a month, France found itself at war with Austria, Britain, Prussia, the Netherlands, and Spain.

Later that year, twenty-two of the more liberal (that is, in this sense, less radical) members of the revolutionary government were executed by a radical faction which had taken control. The period known as the Reign of Terror had begun. Led by a lawyer named Robespierre and his follower Louis Saint-Just, the radicals initiated strict wage and price controls to fight the terrible inflation which raged in France, started universal military conscription to provide for the nation's defense against the armies of Europe which were massing against it, and proceeded to condemn and execute everyone within France whom they saw as their enemy.

Over the next year, the Reign of Terror killed almost twenty thousand French citizens. Although the center of the Terror was in Paris, its tentacles stretched throughout France. At Lyons, for example, some two thousand citizens were killed. At Nantes, between two thousand and six thousand more.

By July of 1794, the frenzy of murder had exhausted itself. Robespierre and Saint-Just were more than willing to continue the Terror, but other, more rational leaders had had enough. Robespierre and Saint-Just were arrested and, along with several of their cohorts, were finally guillotined themselves. The Terror was over, but a great deal of damage had already been done to France, to the Revolution, and to the ideals of liberalism which had inspired it.

Until the Revolution, the execution of Louis XVI, and the Terror, the Enlightenment had carried virtually all the educated men of Europe with it in the direction of liberty, equality, and progressive reform. But these events, as bloody, terrible, and excessive as they seemed, helped to shatter the growing consensus. The result was a much more dramatic split than had existed before between those of essentially conservative and those of essentially liberal points of view.

It would be too simplistic to say that this split divided those who approved of the Revolution and those who disapproved of it. Most men of sense approved of at least some of the goals of the Revolution, while most men of sense also disapproved of at least some of its excesses. But the split did divide those who thought that, for all its faults, the Revolution had accomplished something good and necessary—the freeing of France from a despotic monarchy and an outmoded social system—and those who felt that no tyranny was worse than the tyranny of the mob as exercised by the Revolution itself.

BURKE AND THE
CONSERVATIVE REACTION

The conservative reaction to the events in Europe was most eloquently expressed by Edmund Burke, the British political philosopher and statesman who has been called the founder of modern conservatism. He was, by nature, the prototype of a conservative, in that he had a great respect for tradition coupled with an abhorrence of extreme measures of any kind.

Burke was born in Ireland in 1729. At that time Ireland, which was largely Roman Catholic, was a part of the British Empire. It lived under the often cruel domination of England, which was officially Protestant. A Protestant himself, and devoted to Britain, Burke nonetheless grew up with a deep sympathy for the oppressed Catholics of his native land. He therefore learned very early in life that there may be justice not only on one, but on both sides of an issue. Later, as an important member of the British Parliament, he shied away from supporting drastic governmental measures. Harsh measures, he believed, were justified only when all the right was clearly on the side of the government, a condition that, in his eyes, almost never existed.

Burke's reluctance to support drastic action was not a reluctance to do battle. In fact, he was an unusually combative politician, as often as not, doing battle against his own government. He was particularly determined in his battles to provide better treatment for the subject peoples of the Empire, notably his fellow Irishmen and the native population of India. He led the fight to impeach the first British governor-general of India, whom he believed to be guilty of extortion and of mistreatment of the Indian people.

These elements of his character—his natural conservatism combined with combativeness—meant that he was rarely on the majority's side in any fight and, therefore, rarely on the winning side. He was a man of determined independence of mind, who said of himself: "I believe in any body of men in England. I should have been in the minority. I have always been in the minority."

*Edmund Burke, the British politician
and spokesman for the conservative
reaction to the French Revolution*

By the middle of the eighteenth century, Burke was firmly established in the minority among European intellectuals pertaining to many of the ideals of the Enlightenment. He attacked the skepticism on religious questions which was fashionable at the time, and the idea that man could design, by rational thought, a new and better form of government than that which had grown up organically, naturally, over the centuries.

For Burke, Rousseau's view of man as naturally good and happy, perverted only by the unnatural social institutions which had been formed over a period of time, was exactly backward. Burke was an Anglican Protestant and a believer in original sin. Man was born not good but sinful. Far from being perverted by his social institutions, he was saved by them. It was precisely the institutions of the church and the state which restrained man, which allowed him to overcome the natural defects in his nature.

Burke was a believer in liberty, but it wasn't the unrestrained liberty preached by some of the followers of Rousseau. Nor was it the broadly defined liberty of the Rights of Man, which stopped only where the liberties of others began to be interfered with. Burke's liberty had to be tempered with both "widsom" and "virtue." Without them, Burke argued, liberty is not a positive good at all, but just the opposite. "It is the greatest of all possible evils, for it is folly, vice, and madness, without tuition or restraint."

The wisdom and virtue necessary to turn liberty from "the greatest of all possible evils" into a great good were contained, for Burke, in the very institutions that the "enlightened" followers of Rousseau attacked. Those institutions had grown up as the result of natural processes. Those processes had been set in motion, and guided over centuries, by a force much greater than the feeble mind of any man or group of men, or even of any single generation of men. That force was beyond the capacity of human reason to even understand, much less to better. The idea that any group of men could design something superior to what that force had achieved over centuries was a dangerous and foolhardy one.

It wasn't that reform, or any bettering of social and political institutions, was impossible. Burke was, in fact, in favor of reform, as his various stands against his own government's policies proved. But that reform had to be organic, it had to grow out of the traditions of the past, and not destroy them. It had to be evolutionary, slow, and cautious, and not revolutionary, sudden, arbitrary and capricious. It had to be part of a growing process, and not a tearing up of the roots. "A disposition to preserve and an ability to improve," he wrote, "taken together, would be my standard of a statesman."

Like Hobbes, Locke, and Rousseau, Burke believed in the social contract. But Burke's view of the social contract was more sweeping and majestic than that envisaged by the others. While they had argued, in esssence, that the social contract was an agreement between the people, and classes, of a society to join together in certain political associations for the common good, Burke argued that the social contract actually involved much more than that. "It becomes," he wrote, "a partnership not only between those who are living," (as the others had held) "but between those who are living, those who are dead, and those who are to be born."

This epic view, not only of history, but of the present itself, was basic to Burke's view of reality. For him, society was not something that existed in the present alone. Generations alive, dead, and yet to be born were all linked in a grand design. The preservation of what was good in traditional values and in traditional institutions was something that the present owed to both the past and the future. But it was also something that the present owed to itself. Only through preserving those traditional values and institutions could stability, order, and even civilization itself be saved.

For Burke, one of the great rocks upon which that civilization was built was property, and the natural defenders of that civilization were the men who owned property. They were, he felt, the "proper chieftains" of society, the bearers of the tradition necessary to bind society together.

Conversely, one of the great dangers to that civilization was excessive democracy. It would be a great mistake, he felt, if too much political power was put into the hands of people without property. Aside from questions of education or breeding, those without property simply did not have enough of a stake in the society to be reliable guardians of it.

"All direction of public humour and opinion must originate in a few," he wrote. Those few, of course, were the aristocracy, the landowners. They would, naturally, out of their own best interests, act to preserve the traditional values of the society. It was very clear to Burke that those values had to be preserved, both because they were, as he saw it, "natural" and because if they were not preserved, the result would be chaos, destruction, and human suffering.

The French Revolution, Burke saw immediately, had no interest in preserving those values whatsoever. It was, to the contrary, designed to destroy them.

"The property of France," he wrote in alarm in 1790, "does not govern it." By that he meant that the men of property, those with a real and organic stake in the welfare of the nation, were no longer in control. "In France," he went on, "a cruel, blind and ferocious democracy . . . carried all before them; their conduct, marked with the most savage and unfeeling barbarity . . . manifested no other system than a determination to destroy all order, subvert all arrangement, and reduce every rank and description of men to one common level."

His *Reflections on the Revolution in France*, written in that same year, was the first and most influential literary expression of the conservative response to the Revolution.

Written long before the execution of the king, and even longer before the Reign of Terror, it predicted with amazing accuracy much of what was to follow.

Such a violent overthrowing of tradition, he predicted, would lead to chaos. Such a "ferocious democracy" would lead not to truly representative government, but to despotism. This would come about because when the men of property ceased to govern, when all custom had been overthrown and the organic development of society had been uprooted, the breakdown in order would be unbearable. Sooner or later, that order would have to be restored, and only a despot, backed by military force, would have the power to restore it. Therefore, Burke predicted, the Revolution would ultimately result in the oppression of a military dictatorship. In 1799, in fact, the constitutional government of France fell to a military coup led by Napoleon Bonaparte. Although by his own lights Napoleon continued to carry on many of the aims of the Revolution, the coup seemed to confirm Burke's belief that such a revolution could not lead to an orderly democratic society without the use of military force.

Burke's *Reflections* had an enormous impact both in Britain and abroad. It is still regarded by many as the finest expression of conservative political theory ever written.

While Burke was the most important conservative thinker of his time, he was not alone, either in his revulsion at what took place in France or in his devotion to traditional values. In 1796, Joseph de Maistre, a diplomat and political philosopher from Savoy (now a part of France) published his *Considerations on France*. Prompted by Burke's *Reflections*, de Maistre's work presented a similar but more radically conservative point of view, one which was as influential on much of the continent as Burke's view was in the English-speaking world.

Unimpressed by written constitutions, de Maistre held that the form of government of a country had to grow naturally out of the traditions and national character of that country. It couldn't be imposed according to some abstract theory. As far as France itself was concerned, de Maistre believed that the natural form of government for it was monarchy. Therefore he favored a restoration of the monarchy. As a sop to the revolutionary spirit, he suggested that councils be set up to act as checks on the power of the king, although the membership in those councils would be determined by men chosen by the king himself.

At heart, however, de Maistre was an authoritarian and favored an almost unchecked monarchy. In this, he was quite different from Burke, for whom the monarch was only a useful device. The ruler needed to assure that the system functioned effectively. For de Maistre, the monarch was a "master," and his subjects were obliged to "serve him absolutely."

The authority of the monarch had to be enforced ruthlessly. Unlike Burke, de Maistre didn't believe in reform. Louis had tried reform in France, and the result had been chaos.

The intellectuals of the Enlightenment had helped to spread discontent, and had taught the dangerous doctrine of reform. Consequently, intellectuals should be especially distrusted. (This was an ironic position for de Maistre to take, since he was one of the leading intellectuals of his time, a man of great learning and of brilliant mind.)

Although the monarch was a "master" and had to be served "absolutely," the monarch's power was not absolute. There was one authority above the king, one avenue of appeal against the actions of an unjust sovereign—the pope of Rome. This was another difference between Burke and de Maistre. While both were traditionalists in religion and based their political philosophies firmly on their religious beliefs, de Maistre was much more insistent in the connections he made between his religious and his political views.

For de Maistre, the hand of tradition, the force which had shaped the political institutions of his time, was the hand of God. And, as a Catholic, de Maistre believed in the pope's earthly authority as God's representative on earth. Therefore the pope was the ultimate authority, even above the king.

In de Maistre's ideal world, each nation would have the form of government best suited to its own national character and tradition, but all would be united in Christian submission to the authority of the pope. It would be a world of order and peace and acceptance of the will of God. It was a very appealing world to many conservative-minded Catholics in Europe, particularly in the wake of a revolution which had been so virulently anticlerical, and perhaps even anti-Church.

So it was that the French Revolution became the main crossroads at which the paths of modern liberalism and modern conservatism diverged. Before it, there had been no great division between liberal and conservative political philosophers. Most of the Enlightenment theorists thought of themselves as scientists, not as politicians. They were not being politically conservative or liberal; they were simply trying to find the objective truth. But the French Revolution was such a momentous and overwhelming event that it forced a division. It had, in effect, destroyed the past of a great nation. Now thoughtful men everywhere were divided into those who mourned that past and dreaded what had replaced it, and those who saw in the old system's destruction the best hope for the future of mankind.

But the French Revolution was not the first great liberal revolution. That had taken place a decade earlier, across the Atlantic Ocean, in the American colonies of the British Empire.

3

LIBERALS AND CONSERVATIVES IN AMERICA

The American Revolution, like the French, was deeply rooted in the liberal ideas of the Enlightenment. Its leaders shared many of the concerns and beliefs of the French *philosophes*. They had the same beliefs in progress and in the improvability not only of society but of humanity itself. They had the same fascination with science and the same confidence that the principles of science could be used to improve people's happiness. They shared the same tendency toward democratic principles, although many of them were extremely distrustful of democratic forms of government.

The Declaration of Independence, the document which both announced and justified the Revolution, was a clear product of the liberal Enlightenment. In drafting it, Thomas Jefferson appealed to the same authority so dear to the European theorists, the concept of natural rights—"natural" in the sense that they proceeded from the originator of nature, God, the Creator.

"We hold these truths to be self-evident," he wrote, "that all men are created equal; that they are endowed by their Creator with . . . unalienable rights." The rights that were enumerated—"life, liberty and the pursuit of happiness"—were very similar to the three basic rights set forth by John Locke and later enshrined in the French Declaration of the Rights of Man. The first two, life and liberty, were identical. Jefferson changed the third from "property" to the "pursuit of happiness."

He went on to argue that governments were formed to secure those rights, and that those governments derived "their just powers from the consent of the governed." It was a fundamentally liberal idea. The just powers of a government derived not from divine right, nor from heredity,

This engraving shows Benjamin Franklin, Thomas Jefferson, John Adams, and other members of the committee that drafted the Declaration of Independence.

not even from military might, but from the "consent" of the people. That is, from a social contract.

He then declared that "whenever any form of government becomes destructive of [the liberties of the people], it is the right of the people to alter or abolish it. . . ." In other words, the people had the right to revolution, to throw out the old social contract, and to draw up a new one more to their liking. That, of course, is exactly what they did.

THE NEW CONTRACT

The new social contract drawn up in the wake of the American Revolution was the Constitution of the United States. While the Declaration of Independence had been a fundamentally liberal document, the Constitution reflected a combination of liberal and conservative interests. Although these interests were many and complex, they can be summed up in two overriding concerns: the desire to assure that the new American government would never degenerate into tyranny, and the need to maintain order. The first of these can be described as primarily a liberal concern, while the second is essentially conservative. It would be a mistake, however, to separate those two goals— the desire for freedom and the desire for order—too widely. For most of the framers of the Constitution, they went together. But it is useful in understanding why our governmental system was set up the way it was—to realize that it emerged from a tension between the liberal desire for individual freedom from governmental control and the conservative desire for stability and social order.

The need for stability among the newly independent colonies as well as within them required, or so it seemed to most of the revolutionaries, some form of overall government. About the need for governments for each of the new states, there was never any real question. The American revolutionaries were not anarchists. Each of the former colonies would need a government of its own to make its laws and to keep order within its borders. But whether to establish a general government—one which could exercise power of its own over the citizens or over the several states—was a serious question. Ultimately, that question was settled in what, in the context of the time, was a conservative manner. There would, in fact, be a federal government, one which would exercise power directly over the citizens of the several states.

The other main question, how to prevent the new government from replacing the tyranny of the crown with a tyranny of its own, was a difficult one. It was made more difficult by the fact that possible tyranny came from two sources. The first, paradoxically, was the people themselves.

The people were now sovereign, and the general will would prevail. But the people could easily become a mob. And, as the framers of the Constitution understood very well, the general will could be as destructive to the rights of the individual as the will of the king. Clearly, under this new, more democratic government, ways had to be found to protect the rights of individuals from the tyranny of the majority.

On this issue, perhaps more than any other, the differences between the more liberal and the more conservative of the revolutionaries became clear. Those like Alexander Hamilton and John Adams, who tended to be conservative, had a fairly pessimistic view of human nature. They deeply distrusted the unguided will of the majority. Those of a more liberal bent, most notably Thomas Jefferson, felt that the people had the right to exercise power over their own government. There was, in a sense, no question of trusting them or distrusting them—they were sovereign. Their right to control their own government was "unalienable." It could not be transferred.

Liberals were more concerned about the danger coming from the other direction. If too much of a barrier was put

43

up between the people and the decisions affecting their lives, then what was there to restrain the men in charge of maintaining that barrier? If the government was given power of its own, apart from that resting in the people, then there was a real danger that the men who exercised that power would become dictators.

The document which emerged from the Constitutional Convention, which met in Philadelphia in 1787, was an attempt to meet these differing concerns. Its stirring Preamble set down a combination of conservative and liberal objectives which the government it established was designed to fulfill:

"We, the people of the United States," it began, "in order to form a more perfect union, establish justice, insure domestic tranquillity, provide for the common defense, promote the general welfare, and secure the blessings of liberty to ourselves and our posterity, do ordain and establish this Constitution for the United States of America."

All those objectives were clearly adhered to by both liberals and conservatives. However, the desire to form a more perfect union, to insure domestic tranquillity, and to provide for the common defense were the prime concerns of the conservatives, while establishing justice, promoting the general welfare, and securing the blessings of liberty were uppermost in the minds of the liberals.

The government established by that remarkable document was to be a republic. That is, it would be a democratic government, deriving its authority from "the people," but it would not be a direct democracy, with the masses of the people making its decisions through direct vote. Instead, a broadly based electorate (limited in the beginning mostly to free, propertied, white males) would elect representatives to make those decisions on their behalf and to conduct the public business.

There would be a president, to serve as the chief executive officer of the country and as commander in chief of the armed forces, but his powers were severely limited. There was to be no mistaking the American president for a king, and no chance of his making himself a dictator. He had no authority either to make laws or to levy taxes. Both authorities were delegated, by the people, to their representatives.

The Constitution established a complex system of checks and balances, based on a separation of powers between the various levels and branches of government. The first and most general separation was that between the powers of the federal government and those of the governments of the individual states. But there were other separations even within the federal government itself, the most general of which were those between the executive, legislative, and judicial branches. And even within the legislative branch alone, powers were divided between two distinct houses.

All of this was designed to make it impossible for any branch of the government to get too much power. While the new country was starting out with a generally liberal and optimistic view of man, there was among the framers of the Constitution enough conservative pessimism about man's nature to insure the inclusion of strict protections against the abuse of governmental power. Where power over others was concerned, even the most liberal of the founding fathers, Thomas Jefferson, was conservative. In such matters, he wrote, "let no more be heard of confidence in man, but bind him down by the chains of the Constitution."

The Constitution then, reflected both conservative and liberal values. On balance, however—and in the context of a liberal revolution—it was probably more responsive to conservative concerns than to liberal ones. At least, during the debates which took place over its ratification, it was the conservative leaders, led by Alexander Hamilton, who argued most strongly for its adoption.

Many of the liberals feared that it gave the national government too much power, that there was too much representation and not enough direct democracy. They feared, too, that there was not enough protection of individual rights. They argued that some sort of Declaration or Bill of Rights should be added, spelling out the individual's rights under the new government, and forbidding the government to violate those rights. Jefferson, who took no part in the Constitutional Convention himself, since he was in France as American ambassador at the time, was among those with the strongest doubts. He might even have opposed ratification of the Constitution if an agreement hadn't been made with the conservatives that a Bill of Rights would quickly be added after ratification.

That Bill of Rights was, in fact, added in the form of amendments within a few years after the adoption of the Constitution. It included guarantees of such rights as freedom of religion, speech, and the press; the freedom to assemble and to petition the government for the redress of grievances; freedom from unreasonable search and seizure of one's person or property; the right to a speedy trial and to be free from compulsion to testify against oneself; and the right not to have one's property taken away by the government without "just compensation." All of these guarantees were, in a sense, limitations on the power of the government, and all of them were of special and deep concern to the liberal elements of the new nation.

In the beginning, then, it was the conservatives who wanted the federal government to have greater powers, while it was the liberals who were most concerned to put limits on the power of the government. This came out of the conservatives' desire that the government have enough authority to maintain order, and out of the liberals' concern that the citizens' individual liberties be protected both against the mob and against the government itself.

THE EMERGENCE OF
POLITICAL PARTIES

At first, there weren't any political parties. The majority of the founders didn't want there to be any. They saw parties as means for factions—particular groups of people united either by ideology or just self-interest—to grab power for themselves, to the disadvantage of society at large. They believed each political conflict that came up should be resolved on its own merits, through appeals to reason and, finally, reliance on the will of the people.

Eventually, however, both ideology and self-interest proved too strong for those good intentions, and political parties developed. When they did, they grew up along ideological—liberal and conservative—lines. The first to emerge was the Federalist Party, a conservative faction uniting around the figure of the brilliant first secretary of the treasury, Alexander Hamilton. Their liberal opponents rallied around the equally brilliant first secretary of state, Thomas Jefferson. At first they were called simply the Anti-Federalists, but later, after many name changes, they became known as the Democrats.

Many of the issues over which the Federalists and Anti-Federalists clashed in the first years of the republic continue, in one form or another, to divide conservatives and liberals today. On some of these issues, the two sides have remained consistent over the years; on some, their positions have changed and developed as the country itself has changed.

LAISSEZ-FAIRE
AND STATES' RIGHTS—
CHANGING SIDES

In two major areas—the questions of government interference in the business economy, and of states' rights versus federal rights—liberals and conservatives have, in effect, changed places. The early liberals believed that the government should have little role in the economy. This policy was known as laissez-faire (from a French phrase meaning "let alone to do"), and was set out most clearly in a book entitled *An Inquiry into the Nature and Causes of the Wealth of Nations*, by the Scottish economist Adam Smith. One of the watershed books of the Enlightenment, *The*

47

Wealth of Nations was published in Glasgow in the year of the Declaration of Independence, 1776. In it, Smith argued two main points, both of which were subscribed to by the liberals: first, that the value of goods came from the labor expended on their production; and second, that in a free economy the collective result of the many separate decisions made by all the businessmen and consumers in that economy would be the economic well-being of the society as a whole. He believed that there was what he called an "invisible hand" operating in a free economy, and that if each individual acted in his own economic self-interest, that "invisible hand" would direct the economy as a whole more wisely than any government could direct it. Consequently, the government should adopt a laissez-faire policy and let the individual citizens alone to produce and distribute the nation's goods.

While Jefferson and the liberals favored laissez-faire, Hamilton and the conservatives felt that the government should be directly involved in the nation's economy. The conservatives favored a strong national bank, a strong national currency, and government policies that promoted trade and commerce.

The conservatives tended to see the health of the nation as being very much the same as the health of the economy. More than that, they saw the health of the economy as being very much the same as the health of business in the country. Business, after all, provided not only profit, but jobs. They would have agreed with the Republican president Calvin Coolidge who later expressed the thought suc-

Alexander Hamilton, the first
Secretary of the Treasury, was
a leader of the Federalist Party,
which opposed Jefferson's
Republican party.

49

cinctly: "The business of America," he said, "is business."

Naturally enough, the conservatives looked to government to both promote and protect the business interests that were so essential to the nation. But as time went on, the nature of business in America changed. It got bigger and better able to promote and protect its own interests.

At the same time, government, which had been protecting it, began, under the influence of such men as Theodore Roosevelt and other liberals, to exert more and more control over it. This, the conservatives felt, was hurting both business and the economy in general. Consequently, as liberals became more and more concerned with using government to control and regulate big business, the conservatives became more and more concerned with keeping the government out of business affairs. By 1979, then, the conservative Ronald Reagan was campaigning on a pledge to get government "off the back" of business.

Similarly, the early conservatives had believed in a strong national government. The state governments, they felt, were too small, too contentious, too easily controlled by the irrational prejudice of the citizens of a single state. Only a strong national government could assure domestic and economic tranquillity.

The early liberals, on the other hand, favored a weak national government and strong state governments. They believed that the closer the government was to the people, the more easily controlled by popular will, the better. (For most Americans, of course, their state government was geographically nearer and much more easily controllable than the Federal government.) But, as the federal government became more and more liberal in its policies, conservatives began to turn more and more to the state governments to work their own will. Conversely, the liberals began to favor giving more and more power to the federal government. In the wake of the Civil War, Southern conservatives turned to the states to pass laws that would protect their society from the force of federal laws trying to improve the position of the freed slaves.

With the New Deal, which will be discussed later in this chapter, liberals turned to the federal government to provide the relief the state governments could not provide.

As a result of all this, a kind of flip-flop of positions occurred between the liberals and the conservatives on the questions of states' rights and the government's role in the business economy. It should be pointed out, however, that the underlying desires and concerns of the liberals and the conservatives remained the same. The conservatives embraced states' rights because in doing so they were better able to defend those values of social order and stability that were so dear to them. The liberals embraced a strong federal government because in doing so they found an agent of reform that could better promote the freedoms and social changes that were so dear to *them*. Although their changes in position on these issues may seem somewhat inconsistent, it was, on the contrary, deeply consistent with their most ingrained values.

FIRST AMENDMENT RIGHTS AND NATIONAL SECURITY

One of the consistently recurring subjects of contention between liberals and conservatives throughout American history involves the tension between the rights of the individual—particularly the First Amendment rights of freedom of the press and freedom of speech—and the demands of national security. While both liberals and conservatives support the First Amendment in principle, liberals have consistently applied it more broadly than have conservatives. This fact proceeds from the liberals' traditional tendency to favor individual freedoms over concerns for public order when there seems to be a conflict between the two. Conservatives, on the other hand, have tended to be willing to put more limits on such freedoms in the general interest. This willingness stems from their traditional tendency to value order and security above individual rights, a tendency which can be traced back at least as far as Hobbes.

The first major dispute along these lines came very early in the nation's history, with the passage of the Alien and Sedition Acts in 1798. At that time the conservative Federalists were in power, and they were being heavily criticized by the liberal Jeffersonians for many of their policies. The Federalists were alarmed by the violent excesses of the French Revolution and angered by the Jeffersonians' sympathy for the French. In control of the Congress, the Federalists passed a series of acts aimed at undercutting the liberals. The most important of these was the Sedition Act, which made virtually any criticism of the Congress, the president, or the government in general a criminal offense. They argued that such criticism in a time of international danger was seditious.

A number of Jeffersonians were convicted and jailed under the Act. Most were newspaper editors who had done nothing but write editorials hostile to the Federalists. Liberals objected strongly to the Act, arguing that the First Amendment protected the editors. The conservatives argued that the Amendment couldn't be used as a license to undermine confidence in the government.

The conflict over the Sedition Act was just one of many such conflicts in the course of American history, particularly in times of war. Abraham Lincoln, for example, was accused by his conservative opponents of being a traitor for his opposition to the United States' invasion of Mexico in the 1840s.

Following World War II, a great wave of hostility toward America's wartime ally the Soviet Union swept through the United States. Many people believed that agents of Soviet communism had infiltrated all layers of American society. A number of people and agencies, both in the government and outside it, undertook investigations to discover communists and communist-sympathizers in the United States. Chief among these was Senator Joe McCarthy of Wisconsin. Thousands of Americans were investigated; many lost their reputations, and some lost their jobs after having been accused of being "red" (communist) or "pink" (sympathetic to communists). Most liberals (though not all) argued that these investigations, which often accused people without proof, were unfair and un-American. Citizens, they said, had a right to their own political views, even if they were leftist, and if they weren't proven guilty of a crime, they shouldn't be publicly accused or even lose their jobs for what were alleged to be their political beliefs. Most conservatives (though not all) applauded the efforts of the "commie-hunters." They argued that the nation's security was paramount, and that freedom of political beliefs didn't extend to support of "enemy ideologies" like communism.

Again, at the time of the Vietnam War, in the 1960s and early '70s, the old conflict broke out. Opponents of American involvement in that war (some of them liberal, some radical) staged large demonstrations in the streets to protest the war. Many young men refused to participate in the wartime draft that selected men to go and fight in the war. Many liberals (though far from all) supported the demonstrators, and even the draft-resisters, saying that they had a right both to hold their beliefs about the war and to act on them. Most conservatives, on the other hand, were angry with the demonstrators. Many argued that those who said their government was wrong in Vietnam and that the North Vietnamese (whom the U.S. was fighting) were right, were traitors and had no right to express such beliefs.

SLAVERY

The most emotional issue dividing liberals and conservatives during the nation's early years was the issue of slavery. The liberals, in general, opposed it as being fundamentally repugnant to the principle of individual freedom. Although an owner of slaves himself, Jefferson attempted to put a denunciation of the slave trade into the Declaration of Independence. It was taken out in order to avoid offending the Southern plantation owners. For the same reason, a liberal move to put an article banning slavery into the Constitution was defeated at the Constitutional Convention in 1787.

The issue of slavery continued to work away at the social contract like a worm in the heart of the republic. It came to the fore again in the mid-nineteenth century when it had to be decided whether slavery should be allowed into the new Western territories. Liberals said it should not, while conservatives were willing to go along with the Southern states who argued that it should.

It should be pointed out that while opposition to slavery was a natural outgrowth of liberal philosophy, there was nothing fundamentally conservative about slavery. Many conservatives were personally opposed to the institution. But slavery was an important element in the economy and social structure of the cotton-growing Southern states, and a rough balance of political power existed between the slave states and the free states. Conservatives believed that to abolish slavery, or to forbid its extension into the new territories, would disrupt the economy and social structure of the South, and might upset the delicate political balance of the nation.

One important result of the liberal-conservative conflict over slavery was the formation of the Republican Party, which was founded to oppose the spread of slavery into the territories. Another result, of course, was the Civil War, which settled the slavery question once and for all, although the war itself was much more destructive to the economic, social, and political balance of the country than the mere abolition of slavery which the conservatives had feared would have been.

THE NEW DEAL

The so-called Great Depression of the 1930s brought to the fore one of the main disputes between modern liberals and conservatives—the role of the government in providing for the economic welfare of its citizens.

The Preamble to the Constitution had said that one purpose of the government was "to promote the general welfare," but that aim had been largely interpreted passively. That is, it had been widely interpreted to mean that the government should promote that welfare by providing a healthy economic environment within which people could work for their own private economic good.

But, when the stock market crumbled in 1929 and the nation sank into an economic depression, it seemed clear that both government and private business had failed to provide that kind of healthy economic environment. By 1933, fully one-third of the labor force of the United States was jobless, and the gross national product had been cut almost in half.

By and large, the conservatives believed that the government had to ride out the economic crisis without taking any drastic measures. There had been depressions before, and they had always eventually worked themselves out. Prosperity had always returned. But no earlier depression had been nearly as severe, or lasted nearly as long. It seemed clear to the liberals that something had to be done to help the sixteen million unemployed and their families to survive.

Under President Franklin D. Roosevelt, a liberal-controlled Congress enacted a sweeping collection of economic legislation, called the New Deal, designed to provide financial relief for the suffering victims of the depression, and economic recovery for the nation as a whole. Large government projects were started to provide jobs for the unemployed. New government agencies were formed to regulate agriculture and big business to attempt to get them to operate more productively in the public interest. A minimum wage was established for workers engaged in interstate commerce (it was twenty-five cents an hour), and a maximum work week was legislated for such workers. The federal tax system was reformed. And, most significantly of all, the Social Security system was established to provide unemployment and retirement insurance for American workers.

Conservatives argued that all of this inserted the federal government too deeply into the private financial affairs of individuals. Some even claimed that such measures were sure to destroy the free enterprise system under which the American economy had grown and flourished prior to the Great Depression. Besides, they argued, the huge federal expenditures necessary to fund all these programs would place a crushing tax burden on the citizenry. What's more, the government would have to go so deeply into debt that the economy would be crippled for decades. They challenged much of the New Deal in court, and eventually the Supreme Court declared some of the more radical of its programs unconstitutional.

But most of the New Deal was not only constitutional, it was extremely popular—particularly with those Americans who had been hardest hit by the depression. And it firmly established a major role for the federal government in providing for the private economic welfare of the citizens of the United States, a role the government has not relinquished to this day. Many conservatives still regret that the government ever assumed such a role; others feel that, while the government should have some role in helping the unemployed and the severely disadvantaged, that role has grown much too large and should be drastically cut back.

4

WHAT THEY'VE DONE– LIBERALS AND CONSERVATIVES IN POWER

The New Deal was an exception to the norm of modern American political history. In a few years at the beginning of Franklin D. Roosevelt's administration, an ideological coalition was powerful enough to push through a sweeping program of social and economic reform for the nation.

To understand why this was a rarity in American political life, it's necessary to understand that the machinery of the American government was designed to prevent any temporary ideological majority from taking control of the American government.

The elaborate system of checks and balances established by the Constitution was meant to keep any single group—ideological or otherwise—from gaining too much power. In order for even a single piece of legislation to become law it must pass two separate houses of Congress. The rules of each house are set up in such a way as to make it difficult for any bill to pass quickly or without widespread support within that house. Then, once it has passed both houses, it must be signed by the president. Even after all that, if challenged, it must be certified as being consistent with the Constitution of the United States by the Supreme Court of the United States.

Even the two-party system as it has grown up in this country has worked to make it hard for any ideological group to gain too much power. Both the Democratic and the Republican parties have liberal and conservative wings, as well as many people who consider themselves "in the center." While the Democrats are considered (with some reason) to be inclined to be more liberal on more issues than the Republicans, a Democratic majority in

Congress has rarely assured the passage of liberal legislation. In the same way, a Republican majority has rarely assured the passage of conservative legislation. Neither ideology nor party affiliation is apt to prove decisive when it comes to the passage or failure of important bills in Congress. Each bill's fate is usually decided by the strength of the particular coalition of Democrats and Republicans, liberals and conservatives, supporting it.

The makeup of each such coalition is dependent on many things. Certainly party affiliation plays a part. A congressperson or senator is more apt to support a bill favored by his or her own party's leadership than one favored by the leadership of the other party. Ideology also plays a part. Liberals are more apt to support legislation increasing the federal government's role in assisting the poor, for example, while conservatives are more apt to support legislation limiting that role. But a number of other factors play important parts as well. Among these are geography and the economic forces at work in the politician's home district or state. A bill providing federal money to help America's big cities, for example, will probably be supported by a coalition made up of liberals and conservatives, Republicans and Democrats, who represent large urban areas. It may well be opposed by a coalition of Republicans, Democrats, liberals, and conservatives representing other areas.

Because of all this, it's comparatively rare that any extremely ideological legislation—whether liberal or conservative—is enacted into law. It's even been said that it's harder to enact controversial legislation in the United States than in any other western democracy. It's even harder for any broad program of liberal or conservative measures to be put into effect. Only twice since the New Deal has either ideological group gained enough power to put through something close to a whole program of its own. The first occasion was during the early years of the liberal

Lyndon Johnson's presidency in the 1960s, and the second was during the first years of the conservative Ronald Reagan's presidency, starting in 1981.

LYNDON JOHNSON

The president who preceded Lyndon Johnson in office was, like him, a liberal and a Democrat. He was the young ex-senator from Massachusetts John F. Kennedy. He'd won the presidency in a tight election against the more conservative Republican, Richard Nixon, in 1960. Because the election had been so close, and because the Congress with which he had to work was made up (as usual) of a mixture of Republicans and Democrats of varying degrees of liberalism and conservatism, Kennedy had a great deal of difficulty getting any strongly liberal legislation through the Congress.

Then, on November 22, 1963, Kennedy was assassinated in Dallas and his vice-president, Lyndon Johnson, was thrust into the presidency. Johnson was an old-line New Deal liberal who'd come to Washington as a congressman in a Roosevelt landslide, and who supported the liberal program Kennedy had been trying unsuccessfully to get passed. In the wake of Kennedy's assassination, sympathy for the dead president combined with the political skills of the new one to get that program through.

The presidential election the next year was the most dramatically ideological in the nation's history. The liberal Johnson was opposed by the uncompromisingly conservative senator from Arizona Barry Goldwater. Johnson put forward a broadly liberal program which was designed to build what he called the Great Society, but which Goldwater ridiculed as a "hodgepodge of handouts." Goldwater, true to the conservatives' traditional concern with a strong national defense, indicated that the Democrats were too timid to stand up to the communists. He even suggested that, if he were president, he might be willing to use nuclear weapons in Asia, where American soldiers were already engaged in a war in Vietnam. Such statements, along with his famous proclamation that "Extremism in defense of virtue is no vice," tended to frighten voters. Johnson, meanwhile, campaigned as a "peace candidate."

The result of this clearly defined battle between the liberal Johnson and the conservative Goldwater was a landslide for Johnson and the Democratic Party. The Democrats won 28 out of the 35 Senate seats at stake in the election, as well as 295 of the 435 seats in the House. While not all of these Democrats were ideologically liberal, the majority were, and, combined with the more liberal of the Republicans and the mandate he received in the election, they put Johnson in an almost unprecedented position. He was able to pass through Congress the most liberal program of domestic legislation since the New Deal.

THE WAR ON POVERTY

Johnson exemplified the liberal desire to reform society— to make society better and, through social action, to increase human happiness—a desire that went back at least as far as Rousseau. In the expressed aims of his domestic policies, Johnson was even more ambitious than Franklin Roosevelt had been. He wished, he said, to construct a Great Society, and to eradicate poverty. "This administration," he proclaimed, "here and now declares unconditional war on poverty in America." Having been poor himself, he wished his presidency to be judged, he said, by how many fewer people were poor when he left office than when he entered it.

To that end, he launched a whole series of large and expensive federal programs, the most sweeping since the New Deal. A major new agency, called the Office of Economic Opportunity, was formed to direct the new War on Poverty. Among its many innovations was VISTA (Volunteers In Service To America). Thousands of volunteers, young and old, were sent to poverty-stricken regions of America to help the people there pull themselves out of the cycle of poverty. To help the worst poverty region of all, the Appalachian Mountains, a single act authorized over $1 billion.

Water and Air Pollution acts were passed to help protect the nation's water and air from contamination. The powers of federal regulatory agencies to control the activities of American businesses were increased. The agencies were to use those new powers to keep businesses from unnecessarily endangering the public safety, from harming the environment, and from treating America's consumers unfairly.

Educational reform has long been a concern of liberals (Rousseau, for example, had developed a whole new theory of education), and it was an important part of Johnson's War on Poverty. Over $3.5 billion was earmarked for federal aid to education, including the first federal government scholarships for college students in the history of the country.

Some of the worst poverty in America existed (as it still does) in the slums of the nation's great cities. The War on Poverty attempted to alleviate conditions there by injecting billions of dollars in federal funds for urban renewal and for the development of low-cost housing projects for the poor.

Some of the most lasting measures of Johnson's "War" were in the areas of health insurance and civil rights. For twenty years, American liberals had been fighting to achieve a system of national health insurance. The United States was the only major developed country in the western world which didn't have such a system to provide medical care for its citizens. The idea was bitterly opposed by conservatives, however, led on this issue by a number of powerful professional associations within the medical community. They argued that national health insurance was the first great step toward "socialized medicine" in the

United States, and that would be, in turn, a step toward socialism for the economy as a whole. Under such a system, they claimed, patients would lose the right to choose their own doctors, and health-care decisions would be taken out of the hands of professional medical people and put into the hands of government bureaucrats. Medical care, they claimed, would deteriorate.

Despite strong opposition from the medical societies, and from conservatives in general, Johnson managed to push a $6.5 billion Medicare bill through the Eighty-ninth Congress. That bill provided a limited form of health insurance for Americans over sixty-five, administered by the Social Security Administration. Medicare pays the bulk of a covered elderly person's hospital expenses, and helps to pay some of his or her doctor's bills as well. Although it was far from the complete national health insurance program the liberals wanted, it was a start.

But the most far-reaching reforms to take place under the Johnson administration were in the area of civil rights for America's black citizens. For the century which had passed since the end of the Civil War, the South had effectively stymied the efforts of black people there to exert their political influence, much less to achieve any real social and economic equality. A spider-web system of state laws kept black citizens from most public accommodations; black students from the better schools (which were inevitably the white schools, which received the majority of the funds available for education); black families from white neighborhoods; black business from competing effectively with white businesses; and, most disastrously of all, large numbers of black voters from exercising their right to vote. Subtler methods had much the same effect in many areas of the North. The efforts of the Johnson administration—most notably the Voting Rights Act of 1965— helped to begin to put an end to that. They did much to turn around the century-old pattern of overt racial discrimination and oppression in the United States.

In all, in the first two years of Johnson's full term as president, more than fifty Great Society measures were passed by the Congress. The programs they established added up to a staggering total of federal expenditures. One estimate was that they would end up costing over $122 billion. Conservatives were horrified, not only by the sweeping nature of the changes these programs were designed to bring about in society, but by their enormous cost. "Think of it!" one of them exclaimed. "This spending program dwarfs into utter insignificance all past spending programs, by all nations, all over the world." While that was clearly an overstatement, $122 billion was clearly a lot of money.

It was not, however, enough.

THE "WAR" IS LOST

The War on Poverty failed to eradicate poverty in the United States. It even failed to keep liberals loyal to the man who waged it, Lyndon Johnson. Before his term was out, Johnson announced that he wouldn't try for reelection. He knew he couldn't win. Not because of conservative opposition, which wouldn't have been strong enough to beat him, but because of liberal opposition.

Liberals, who'd voted for the "peace candidate" Johnson against the "hawk" Goldwater, were bitter and angry. Instead of pulling American troops out of the war in Vietnam, he'd drastically escalated American involvement there. (This had demonstrated again something which has often been demonstrated in American politics—that liberals and conservatives tend, once in office, to conduct foreign policy in surprisingly similar ways, whatever their differences in rhetoric.)

Beyond that, however, Johnson's economic policies had failed. He'd combined the expensive prosecution of two "wars," the one against the Communists in Vietnam, and the other against poverty here at home, with what might be considered a conservative measure: a huge excise tax cut. These two elements, the drastically raised federal expenditures and the tax cut, worked against each other, and against the economy.

Liberals blamed Johnson for not having gone far enough in the War on Poverty to win it, and going too far in the war in Vietnam. If he'd spent more money on the "war" at home and less on the war in Asia, the liberals believed, he might have succeeded. The conservatives believed the opposite. They blamed him for going too far in the War on Poverty, and not far enough in the war in Vietnam.

The choice that Johnson faced in trying to prosecute his two "wars" was a classic liberal-conservative dilemma. It was expressed in a metaphor that has become a central part of the language of American politics—a choice between "guns" and "butter." There is a limited amount of money (and of other resources) available for the federal government to expend in accomplishing its many aims. Those measures which relate to the military are known in political shorthand as "guns". Those which are domestic and have to do with improving the quality of life for Americans, particularly those who are poor or otherwise disadvantaged, are referred to as "butter." When deciding whether to spend the nation's resources on guns or butter, many hard choices have to be made. Faced with those choices, conservatives tend to opt for guns, while liberals tend to opt for butter.

In the case of Lyndon Johnson, he couldn't make the hard choice of whether to concentrate the bulk of federal resources on guns (the war in Vietnam) or butter (the War on Poverty). Instead, he attempted to get both guns and butter. He ended up expending huge amounts of money and other resources on both his "wars." Those expenditures in total proved large enough to produce huge government debts (called deficits) and other economic troubles at home, but not large enough to win either of the "wars."

Poverty was not eradicated in the United States, and the war was not won in Asia either.

The greatest liberal opportunity since the New Deal had ended in failure.

RONALD REAGAN AND THE
CONSERVATIVE EXPERIMENT

The conservatives got their chance to take power in 1980 with the election of Ronald Reagan. Like the liberals' earlier opportunity, the conservatives' chance came as the result of misfortune. For the liberals, it was the assassination of a president. For the conservatives, it was a combination of the unpopularity of another president, Jimmy Carter, rampaging inflation, and the long ordeal of scores of American citizens held hostage in Iran. All these factors helped to bring Ronald Reagan, who had picked up Barry Goldwater's mantle as the leading conservative in the Republican Party, into the presidency.

He came with a large electoral victory that was seen as a mandate for his policies. In his first year in office he faced opposition from a confused and demoralized Democratic Party, which lacked the will to strongly oppose him on any important matter. As a result, he had an opportunity much like that which Johnson had enjoyed in 1964—the opportunity to push through a legislative program which was as close to being ideologically pure as seems to be possible under the American system of government. And he took it. He proved as competent to manipulate Congress as Johnson had been, and his actions and his programs as president in his first year in office are the best practical examples available of a modern conservative in action.

It was clear from the start that President Reagan was not going to be another "moderate," as modern Republican presidents, from Eisenhower to Ford, had tended to be. He made dramatic moves early which demonstrated that he

When Ronald Reagan was inaugurated
as president in 1981, he moved
swiftly to implement his conservative
policies in the national economy
and in foreign affairs.

intended his administration to be as conservative as he was himself.

Among those moves were two on the international front, both of which proceeded from the long-held belief of American conservatives that the liberals (and even the moderates) were too gullible and too weak in promoting America's interests in the world at large. Reagan announced that he was not willing to sign two major treaties that previous American administrations had negotiated and agreed on with foreign governments. These were the second Strategic Arms Limitation Treaty (or SALT II), on which American and Soviet representatives had agreed after long and painstaking negotiations, and the Law of the Sea Treaty. The latter had been negotiated by several American administrations, together with some one hundred fifty nations, and was considered by many experts to be the most far-reaching and impressive result of multinational negotiations ever reached. In Reagan's view, however, both these treaties "gave away" too much that was vital to the interests of the United States, and he was determined not to go along with them.

Whatever the merits of the treaties, or of Reagan's objections to them, the president had given clear notice that something new, and fundamentally conservative, was happening in Washington. This was not government as usual.

Where Lyndon Johnson, typically liberal, had believed that the government could and should solve the problems of the nation, Reagan, typically conservative, did not. "Government," he declared, in a formulation which would be heartily agreed with by most conservatives, "is not the solution to our problem. Government *is* the problem." His main domestic priority proceeded directly from this fundamental belief. It was to reduce the size and scope of activities of the American government. In his own terms, to reduce "the problem" that plagued American life.

Internationally, his main priority reflected another major

concern of American conservatives—national defense. To that end, he was determined to increase the strength of America's armed forces, and particularly its nuclear forces. He proposed a massive $1.5 trillion military buildup, the largest in United States history, to take place over five years.

But, while he wanted American defense spending to be increased dramatically, he wanted government expenditures (as well as government activities) in other areas to be reduced equally dramatically. He set to work demolishing a number of federal agencies and slashing the proposed budgets of virtually all the rest. In his own first budget, planned expenditures were cut (often drastically) on some two hundred fifty separate federal programs. Among these were Medicare, Medicaid (which provided limited medical care to the poor), virtually every aspect of the nation's other welfare programs, and even Social Security. Federal funds for education were cut back. Money for the Environmental Protection Agency was reduced, and the activities of it, and many of the other federal regulatory agencies which had been set up to regulate business in the public interest, were curtailed in the name of "getting the government off the backs of American business." The national railway services, Amtrak and Conrail, had their services reduced. Federal funds for research designated to make America more self-sufficient in energy production were lowered. Interest rates on federal loans to the victims of natural disasters were raised. And on and on.

All of these reductions in expenditures were intended to help achieve another major goal of conservative policy, to reduce the burden of taxation. Unfortunately, inflation and the huge increases in the military budget canceled out whatever reductions in expenditures might have occurred as a result of the cutbacks in domestic programs. Nonetheless Reagan proposed—and both the Republican Senate and the Democrat-controlled but disorganized House of Representatives passed—a major cut in personal and business income taxes. Despite the rising federal budget, Reagan believed that he could cut income taxes and still reduce the federal deficit—the amount of money the government had to borrow to pay its debts.

Liberals scoffed at the idea. They argued that if Reagan raised expenditures (primarily the military budget) and lowered income (the money coming in from taxes), he would have to increase the deficit. But Reagan believed, along with the young conservative economist Arthur Laffer, that a tax cut would actually produce *more* income for the federal government, not less. The theory was that if both people and businesses had more money to spend, the businesses would be able to produce more goods, and the people would be able to buy more of those goods. This would result in bigger profits for the businesses, which would in turn employ more people, who would in turn pay more taxes. Even at a lower tax *rate* then, Americans would actually pay more in taxes to the federal government than they would have otherwise. The increase in revenues brought about by the tax cuts, combined with the reductions in social programs, would more than offset the increase in the military budget, Reagan and the conservatives argued. This would result in a balanced federal budget within a few years.

Despite the fact that many members of Congress doubted this theory—even Reagan's vice-president, George Bush, had referred to it as "Voodoo economics" during his own campaign for the Republican presidential nomination—Congress passed most of Reagan's budget, and the tax cut as well. It was time, they believed, to give conservative policies a try.

Reagan's programs were a dramatic assault on the whole direction in which the American government had been moving for decades. It was an effort to return America to many of the policies and principles which had prevailed before the Great Depression had thrown the American ecomony, and American politics, into turmoil. The result of the Depression had been the liberal New Deal, in which the government had taken over much of the responsibility for actively promoting the economic welfare of its citizens. The government had maintained that responsibility ever since. In the Johnson years, it had even increased it. Now, for the first time since the New Deal, there was a real effort by a president not just to slow the liberal movement of the American government, but to turn it around. It was a conservative effort not so much to reform the government as to restore it to what it had been before. And that effort seemed, in the first year of the Reagan administration, to be succeeding. As *U.S. News and World Report* put it: "In little more than five months, Ronald Reagan has reversed a thrust of expanding government that has dominated Washington for nearly a century."

If things had continued to move to the right, unchecked, for the whole of Reagan's presidency, it would have been the most profound transformation of the American government since the New Deal. Perhaps the most profound ever. But, as with Johnson, what Reagan was actually able to do was ultimately not enough to accomplish the hugely ambitious goals he'd set for himself.

At this writing, the Reagan administration is not yet over, and there may be many dramatic developments yet to come. At least some of the achievements of the administration have been dramatic already. Perhaps most significantly, inflation, which had been running high at the time of Reagan's election, and which had surged ahead even stronger for a time thereafter, was down to a moderate four percent by late 1983. The severe recession that had struck the country during Carter's term was also in moderation under Reagan.

And yet, unemployment, one of the most painful elements of that recession, was higher than at the time Reagan and his conservative supporters had taken over. The second year of Reagan's income tax cut was coupled with rises in other taxes which did much to offset it. The burst

71

of new investment and economic activity which the conservatives had predicted failed to develop.

Reagan himself came under increasing criticism from the conservatives for what they saw as too great a willingness to compromise his conservative principles for political advantage. Reagan was finding, as Johnson had found before him, that it is impossible to govern a country like the United States without compromise. And, the more ideological of the conservatives found this compromise as distasteful as the more ideological of the liberals had done. Worst of all—in the eyes of many conservatives—budget deficits had not been reduced. In fact, they had grown steadily throughout the Reagan presidency, setting records as the most massive federal deficits in the history of the country.

But, despite the limitations of its conservative achievements, the Reagan administration has already made an enormous difference in the American government. If it hasn't entirely reversed the thrust of expanding government, as the *U.S. News and World Report* claimed, it has certainly moderated it. More importantly, it has changed many Americans' perceptions of that thrust. It has helped to shift the center of the American political debate sharply to the right. By the congressional election campaigns of 1982, midway through Reagan's term, even liberal Democrats were talking about cutting social programs.

5

WHAT THEY BELIEVE TODAY

Before discussing the major differences in belief between American conservatives and liberals, it's important to discuss some of the profound beliefs they share. While there has always been a deep division between conservatives and liberals in the United States, that division has always been overshadowed by their common beliefs and values. In his first inaugural address, in 1801, Thomas Jefferson, leader of the liberals who called themselves Republicans, proclaimed: "We are all republicans. We are all federalists." And he was right. Despite the great differences between himself and such conservatives as Alexander Hamilton and John Adams, they shared a common loyalty to the federal republic they had helped to establish, and to the values for which it stood. That common loyalty still unites American conservatives and liberals today.

Among the most basic of their common values are these: a commitment to the ideal of freedom; a devotion to the United States itself, and to the Constitution on which its government is based; faith in the nation's future; a belief in private property; and a respect for public order.

Both conservatives and liberals believe that freedom is a fundamental human value. When conservatives demand that the government stop regulating this or that industry, they argue that such regulation is interfering with the freedom of those engaged in that industry. When liberals demand that the government force industries to stop polluting the air, they argue that it must do so to protect people's freedom to breathe pure air. While they might disagree with each other's definition of "freedom," they share a common devotion to the ideal. If the United States has a single founding ideal, that ideal is freedom.

74

Both conservatives and liberals are loyal to the country, and to its government. While both criticize it from their different perspectives and want some things about it changed, both proceed from a belief that it is, ultimately, "the last, best hope of Earth." Conservatives tend to agree more with the nineteenth-century naval officer Stephen Decatur, who declared: "Our country! . . . may she always be in the right; but our country, right or wrong!" Liberals tend to agree more with the liberal secretary of interior Carl Schurz, who said: "Our country . . . when right, to be kept right; when wrong, to be put right." But both take great pride in that phrase "Our country."

Controversies over the Constitution have been some of the deepest and most bitter in American political life. And yet, while both might favor some changes in the document, neither liberals nor conservatives have ever expressed any great desire to throw out the Constitution and start all over again. This devotion to constitutional government, and to the basic document drawn up in Philadelphia nearly two centuries ago, is so ingrained that it's hardly ever thought about. And yet, it's one of the most remarkable facts of American political life.

Almost equally ingrained in the America character is a kind of instinctive faith in the future of the country. It's an essentially liberal faith—growing out of the Enlightenment belief in the improvability of society—but in America it is widely shared by conservatives and liberals alike. The United States has gone through periods of economic turmoil, it's suffered through a murderous Civil War, and in recent years many Americans have been saddened by what they see as a worsening of its position in the world. Yet, few Americans have ever doubted that, in the long run, America would recover from her difficulties and eventually emerge stronger and healthier than ever before.

The right to property has been fundamental to both liberal and conservative thought in the United States from the beginning. It was, in fact, one of the rights for which the American Revolution was fought. The Constitution itself has explicit provisions assuring that no citizen can be deprived of property without "due process of law" and "just compensation," and neither conservatives nor liberals have ever supported any basic change in those provisions.

Nor has either group suggested an overturning of the established political or social order. Liberals believe that a more equitable distribution of resources would be good for the country. Conservatives believe that too many resources have already been taken out of private hands and been redistributed by the government. But neither conservatives nor liberals believe that the system itself should be overthrown. Although the nation was founded in revolution, and most liberals and conservatives alike would agree that people have a right to revolt if their government becomes oppressive, neither group believes that things have ever reached so desperate a condition in the United States.

It may seem strange that people of such differing political philosophies would share so many fundamental beliefs and values. It may seem strange that liberals, who by nature favor change and reform, should remain devoted to a Constitution drawn up nearly two hundred years ago. Thomas Jefferson, after all, believed that a new Constitution, a new social contract, should be drawn up every twenty years. And it may also seem strange that conservatives, who by nature are traditionalists and pessimistic about change and experimentation, should have faith in the future of such an ongoing experiment as the United States of America.

But these paradoxes may be partly explained by another paradox, pointed out by Clinton Rossiter in his book *Conservatism in America*. He points out that the United States was founded on the principles of liberalism. It was born in a liberal revolution, and the Constitution which established its form of government is an essentially liberal document. Consequently, the very *tradition* of the United States consists of the liberal values of freedom, change, and reform. As Rossiter puts it, Americans have traditionally "thought of liberty as a heritage to be preserved rather than as a goal to be fought for." The result, he says, is a political tradition that is "conservative about liberalism."

It is usually the liberals who trace their beliefs back to John Locke, but to some extent American conservatives have a claim on him as well. William F. Buckley, whose magazine, *National Review*, has long been a voice for conservatives, made this point when he referred to Ronald Reagan as "that Lockean in the White House." By that he meant to say that Reagan, and American conservatives in general, believe in the principles of freedom, and particularly freedom from the tyranny of government, traditionally associated with the liberal thought of John Locke.

RADICALS TO
THE LEFT AND RIGHT

To say that liberals and conservatives share the fundamental beliefs and values just mentioned is to say that they occupy the area around the center of the American political spectrum. There are other, more extreme positions on that spectrum. In order to understand what it is that liberals and conservatives believe, it's necessary to make a distinction between their beliefs and the more radical beliefs of those farther out on either side of the political spectrum.

To understand this, it's useful to refer to those political terms which started in use at the time of the French Revolution—right, left, and center. If we think of the American political spectrum as a line, the center of that line represents a kind of nonideological, moderate political position: people who like some of the ways things are and dislike others but who have no clear conviction of what should be done, if anything, to change them.

To the left of that center are the liberals, becoming more intensely liberal the farther to the left you go. Near the center to the left, for example, you find those who approve of most of the current social welfare programs but believe that some should be cut and others changed to make them more efficient. They also, typically, believe that defense expenditures should be trimmed a little bit. Farther left you find those who believe that welfare programs should be expanded and defense spending should be cut dramatically.

Conversely, to the right of the center you find those who believe that some social welfare programs should be trimmed, for example, and others abolished completely. They also typically believe that defense expenditures should be somewhat increased. Further to the right are those who believe that *most* welfare programs should be scrapped while defense expenditures should be increased enormously. These are just examples of a whole range of political views which get gradually more extreme the further out you go on the political spectrum.

At some point in each direction, you reach the limits of liberal and conservative thought and pass on to something more radical. On the left, liberal economic beliefs turn into socialism, and even further, into communism. On the right, conservative economic beliefs turn first into a kind of economic anarchy and finally into a form of state-controlled economy, the descendent, in a way, of the state-run mercantile systems which first replaced feudalism.

On each end of the political spectrum, then, is a form of totalitarianism, a form of government in which the state controls the most important aspects of an individual's life—economic, political, and social. On the left, this is known as totalitarian communism (not all forms of communism are totalitarian); and on the right, it's known as fascism. Each of these is diametrically opposed to the basic ideal of individual liberty. Such traditional American values as freedom of speech and assembly are jettisoned by

78

the totalitarian radicals of both the far left and the far right. Rather than being cherished for everyone, such freedoms are reserved for those whose political views are considered correct. Most such radicals would say that no one has a right to preach error.

When reviewing the political spectrum, it's important to realize that the fact that communism is on the same side of the political spectrum as liberalism does not mean that liberalism is just a step on the way to communism. Nor does the fact that fascism is on the same side of the political spectrum as conservatism mean that conservatism is just a step on the road to fascism. In fact, both liberals and conservatives detest both forms of totalitarianism, not only for their economic principles, but for their assaults on human freedoms.

DIFFERENCES
ON SOCIAL ISSUES

Now that we have looked at some of the beliefs shared by American liberals and conservatives, and some of the beliefs mutually opposed by them, it's time to examine some of the important things about which they differ.

A number of their differences have already been discussed. These include the shifting liberal-conservative positions on laissez-faire economic policies and states' rights, their conflicts concerning public welfare programs, and their differing priorities when an individual's rights under the First Amendment have to be weighed against the interests of national security. But there are a number of other important issues, both domestic and international, which remain to be discussed.

On a whole range of what are often referred to as "social issues," modern-day liberals and conservatives reflect the concerns and priorities traditional to their ideologies. While both groups believe in the importance of both individual liberty and a peaceful, orderly society, the first concern most often seems to take precedence for liberals, while the second takes precedence for conservatives.

Thus, although many conservatives were just as opposed morally to racial segregation in the United States as were many liberals, it was the latter who pressed for the overturning of segregation laws in the South and the passage of the federal Civil Rights and Voting Rights acts in the 1960s.

So, too, while many liberals are just as opposed morally to the use of such drugs as cocaine as are most conservatives, it is the conservatives who are in the forefront of the demand for stricter enforcement of the anti-drug laws.

When it comes to social issues, conservatives (particularly those who sympathize with such Christian-oriented conservative groups as the Moral Majority) tend to favor the passage of laws banning acts which they regard as immoral and destructive, and the stricter enforcement of criminal laws in general.

Examples of such activities, which conservatives feel should be made illegal (or, where they already are illegal, should be more heavily penalized), are these: abortion; pornography; the use of marijuana, cocaine, and other "recreational" drugs; the promotion of sexual life-styles other than monogamous marriage; and the dissemination of literature with strong sexual content, or which they see as containing left-wing political propaganda, particularly through the public schools.

Conservatives favor such laws because they feel that American society is in danger of breaking down. They feel that the activities they oppose have been increasing to such an extent that the traditional values of American life are threatened. Stronger laws are needed, they believe, to protect those values.

Liberals tend to oppose such laws—not, in many cases, because they approve of the activities the conservatives want banned, but because they believe that those activities are matters of personal choice, or personal morality, not

Under the leadership of the liberal president
Lyndon B. Johnson, Congress passed
much legislation dealing with social issues
in the 1960s. Here President Johnson
shakes hands with Martin Luther King, Jr.,
after signing the Civil Rights Act.

matters of law. Many of them, they believe, such as the dissemination of controversial literature, are implicitly protected by the Constitution.

When the conservative Barry Goldwater ran for president in 1964, one of his campaign pledges was that as president he would do something about "crime in the streets." From that time on, what to do about violent crime has become something of a political issue in the United States. Once again, the conservatives are firmly on the side of imposing order. They believe, in general, that the courts have shown too much concern for the rights of people accused of crimes, and not enough concern for the victims of those crimes; that jail sentences for convicted criminals should be harsher; and that the death penalty should be imposed, and carried out, more often.

While liberals are also concerned with the victims of crime, they feel that the courts must continue to show great concern for the rights of the accused. Under American law, a person accused of a crime is to be considered innocent until, and unless, proven guilty. To do otherwise would be to violate the Constitution and to put the entire foundation of American justice in jeopardy.

The prisons are already drastically overcrowded, point out the liberals. To put more people in prison longer would simply aggravate the problem. Besides, imprisoning people under current conditions simply embitters them and makes them more dangerous than ever when they get out.

The death penalty, they say, doesn't deter crime, and to use it puts society in the same position as that of the criminal, using the ultimate form of violence against its enemies.

An interesting exception to the general rule that conservatives tend to favor more, and harsher, criminal laws while liberals tend to oppose them, comes in the area of gun control. Here liberals, noting the widespread use of handguns in violent crime, tend to favor legislation which would make it more difficult, if not impossible, to legally buy and own a handgun. Conservatives, pointing out that the Constitution affirms the right of the people to "bear arms," oppose such legislation.

With the above exception, however, it is clear to see how these modern-day conservative and liberal views on social issues are direct results of traditional conservative and liberal thought. In all of them, the conservatives show their longtime concern for maintaining a peaceful and orderly society based firmly on traditional values. The liberals, on the other hand, show their longtime concern for the freedom of the individual and the need to protect him or her from the tyranny of the majority, as exercised by the government.

Just as dramatic as the differences over economic and social policies, and ultimately perhaps even more vital, are the differences over foreign policy. These divide themselves into three main areas: America's relations with its allies, with the Soviet Union, and with the developing nations of the Third World.

DEALING WITH OUR ALLIES

In our early history, both liberals and conservatives were wary of foreign alliances. While both believed that we should have trade and cultural relations with other countries, they feared that we might become too dependent on other nations, or worse, be drawn into their wars. This is what George Washington meant when he warned against America becoming involved in "entangling alliances."

Today, however, the United States is involved in several "entangling alliances," and both conservatives and liberals support at least some of them. The two do differ signifcantly, however, in their perspectives on those alliances.

Liberals fear that we have too many military alliances, alliances which call on us to come to other nations' defense if they are attacked, in too many parts of the world. While some places—notably Europe, and perhaps Central America—are vital to our national security, other areas—including most of Asia—are not. They feel that we aren't concentrating our limited resources on those areas of the world which are most important to us. They feel that we are making unnecessary dangers for ourselves by becoming committed to too many unstable governments; and that, being spread so thin, we are losing our credibility as a military ally.

Liberals also feel that many of our alliances with other countries are unfair, putting too much of the responsibility for maintaining the other nation's security on us, and bringing us little or nothing of value in return. They feel that our allies around the world should take more of the responsibility for their own defense.

Conservatives share some of these concerns, but their view of where our national security interest may be vitally threatened is much broader than that of the liberals. They see the world as a vast stage on which an ideological battle between the free world, led by the United States, and the communists, led by the Soviet Union, is played out. For them, any demonstration of Soviet power or influence anywhere in the world is a threat to the power and influence of the United States. They feel that, as much as possible, we must help any nation, anywhere in the world, to stay free of communist influence.

Liberals, on the other hand, make more of a distinction between the ideology of communism and the power of the Soviet Union. They believe that, while the Soviet Union is a potential threat to American interests, communism as such is not. Further, they believe that not every example of Soviet power is a danger to us. In other words, liberals have a narrower view of America's strategic interests. Thus, they would lessen our military commitments around the world, confining them to those areas near our borders, or to where it is clear that vital American interests (such as our sources of oil in the Middle East) are directly affected.

In our trading relations with our allies, both liberals and

conservatives agree that we should work toward a more favorable balance of trade. At present, we purchase many more goods from abroad than we sell there. This results in a net loss for American industry, and in a loss of jobs at home. Rather than American companies and workers making goods and selling them abroad, keeping jobs at home and bringing in money from abroad, we are sending more of our own money overseas to pay for goods made by foreign companies, and employing foreign labor. Both conservatives and liberals recognize this problem but they favor different solutions to it. Modern conservatives tend to subscribe to the old liberal policy of laissez-faire, believing that in time American industry will become more competitive, produce goods better and cheaper, and thereby sell more abroad. Liberals, meanwhile, have come to favor more use of protective tariffs, the placing of heavy import fees on goods brought into this country. They have abandoned their earlier support of laissez-faire because of their concern for American workers who have, particularly in the steel and automobile industries, lost great numbers of jobs to foreign competition. The liberals feel that these millions of unemployed must be helped now. There isn't time to wait for American business to turn itself around.

DEALING WITH THE SOVIETS

As mentioned earlier, both liberals and conservatives recognize the Soviet Union as a potential military threat to the United States. Both believe we must be militarily strong enough to meet that threat. But their analyses of the threat, and of how to meet it, are different.

Conservatives see any country with a communist government as a likely ally of the Soviets and a threat to the United States. Many see even those noncommunist countries who have close trading or cultural relations with the Soviets as possible threats. Any country which receives a great deal of assistance from the Soviets, for example, may

The presence of these U.S. advisers in El Salvador
reflects the view that the United States should
provide military assistance and even commit
troops to support friendly governments threatened
by Marxist revolution.

become dependent on them, and therefore might be willing to assist them, even militarily, against the U.S.

Liberals believe that this conservative view of the Soviet military threat is exaggerated. Although they agree that the Soviets present a distinct threat, they feel that most other communist countries, and the Third World countries friendly to the Soviets, do not.

Since they see the Soviet military threat as both massive and widespread, and presenting potential enemies all over the globe, the conservatives feel that a massive military buildup on the part of the United States is needed to meet it. Both America's nuclear triad—the three-legged defense system of nuclear weapons on land, bombers in the air, and submarines under the sea—and its conventional (nonnuclear) forces need to be strengthened. The triad must be strengthened, they argue, because the Soviets have more missiles by far than we have. Conventional forces must be beefed up because the Soviet armed forces are much bigger than ours.

Liberals argue that the military threat is not nearly so great as the conservatives believe. Third World countries, they say, however friendly to the Soviets, present little realistic threat to us. American nuclear forces, they maintain, are at least equal to the Soviets' in overall strength. The Soviets may have more missiles, but the United States has more warheads. Besides, the numbers are so large that which side has more has become irrelevant. Since each has the capacity to destroy the other several times over, what does it matter who has the most? The triad, they say, is invulnerable. Though the Soviets may be able to destroy the land-based leg, the bombers and submarines would still be safe.

Even the supposed superiority in conventional forces which the Soviets hold is misleading, the liberals argue. True, they have twice as many soldiers as the United States, but they need their large army to counter the potential threat to themselves from their hostile neighbor to the east, China, and not for some hypothetical attack on the West.

These differences in analyses result in liberals' and conservatives' taking different approaches to a number of issues, including military expenditures and nuclear disarmament. The conservatives, believers in holding down the expenditures of the federal government in most respects, tend to be big spenders when it comes to weaponry. Since they see the military threat as immediate and virtually worldwide, they tend to favor almost any expansion of American military might, whether nuclear or conventional, to meet it. Liberals, who see the threat as smaller, argue in favor of holding down military expenses wherever feasible.

Both groups speak in favor of nuclear disarmament, but, in practice, liberals tend to support measures aimed at achieving such disarmament while conservatives tend to oppose them. A good illustration of this is the recent move to promote a nuclear freeze, in which both the United States and the Soviet Union would stop building any new nuclear weapons. Several referenda supporting such a freeze have been put on ballots around the country. Although the freeze is described on those ballots as being "mutual" (meaning that both the U.S. and Soviets would have to agree to it before it would go into effect) and "verifiable" (meaning that it would be monitored so that each side would be sure that the other side was keeping to it), conservatives have tended to oppose the referenda, while liberals have tended to support them.

Conservatives say that, however the referenda are stated, such a freeze could not be verifiable and the Soviets would be sure to cheat. Liberals say that the freeze agreement could be drawn up in such a way as to make sure that the Soviets couldn't cheat. People who consider themselves "experts" on weaponry have supported both sides. Since most ordinary citizens lack the knowledge on which to base a sound judgment as to whether such a freeze could be truly *scientifically* verifiable or not, positions on the freeze issue tend to boil down to a matter of political temperament. Conservatives, reflecting the traditional conservative pessimism, say no; liberals, reflecting the traditional liberal optimism, say yes.

DEALING WITH
THE THIRD WORLD

Some of the strongest differences between liberals and conservatives come into focus when dealing with questions relating to the developing countries of the Third World. Although these countries are, by definition, allies of neither the United States nor the Soviet Union, the fear of the spread of Soviet power dominates the conservatives' thinking about them. As Norman Podhoretz, who is a leading conservative when it comes to this issue, expresses it: "I think any extension of Soviet power, almost anywhere in the world, is contrary to the interests of the United States. . . . In theory, I would wish to prevent the Soviet Union from extending its power and influence even another inch beyond [where] that power and influence already prevails." He acknowledges that this "ideal policy" cannot be successfully pursued everywhere in the world, but argues that it must be pursued to the extent possible, everywhere possible. Most conservatives agree.

The main goal of a conservative foreign policy vis-à-vis the Third World, then, is to prevent the spread of Soviet (or communist) influence. To this end, conservatives believe the United States should help strengthen anticommunist governments around the world so that those governments can fight communism both within their own countries and outside them. To some extent, this help could be economic, but for the most part, it would be military.

Liberals do not necessarily disagree that governments fighting communism elsewhere in the world should be supported, although they usually favor a lower level of aid than the conservatives do. Where liberals and conservatives come into sharp disagreement on this issue, though, is when the government asking for help is a dictatorship, unpopular with its own citizenry, that wants American help to put down its own people. In these cases, the liberals argue, the United States has no business helping the government at all. The United States, they say, was born in a revolution itself. It would be ideologically and morally wrong to fight one form of totalitarianism (communism) by supporting another form of totalitarianism (the existing repressive dictatorship).

Another difference often surfaces when the help offered to a Third World government comes in the form of covert (or secret) activity on the part of the American Central Intelligence Agency (the CIA).

Liberals argue that such activities are illegal, both under American law and (most often) under the laws of the Third World country in which they take place. Conservatives counter that no law takes precedence over a nation's right to defend itself. The United States, they say, is in a war with communism and has a right to employ whatever means are necessary to win that war.

Liberals claim that covert action is almost always unsuccessful. Furthermore, on those occasions when it has come to light, it has been an intense embarrassment both to the United States and to the friendly foreign government involved. Conservatives claim that covert action by the CIA has often, in fact, been successful. Those occasions, however, have to remain secret. The CIA, they say, is in the unfortunate position of having its failures exposed for public ridicule, while being unable to tell anyone about its successes.

Another major reason liberals tend to be more reluctant to grant military help to unpopular foreign governments is that they believe that such help is often counterproductive. Truly unpopular governments, they argue, are bound to fall sooner or later. If the United States has tried to bolster up the unpopular government before its fall, then the new government that takes its place will almost certainly be hostile to the United States. It may well turn to the Soviet Union for help. Therefore, the liberals argue, too often in our effort to prevent a country from going communist, we have in effect driven that country into the communist camp ourselves.

While liberals tend to oppose large-scale military aid to Third World countries, they often support aid of other kinds, particularly agricultural and economic. These kinds of assistance, which help to combat the effects of poverty in the developing countries, are, they claim, the best defense against the spread of communism there. Communism feeds on poverty, getting its recruits from the ranks of the impoverished. Make life better for the residents of a poor country, the liberals say, and you make the possibility of a communist revolution less likely.

Conservatives agree that this sounds attractive in theory, but they contend that it doesn't work in practice. "I think the record of economic aid to Third World countries . . . is a dismal one," Norman Podhoretz says. "The record, now reaching back for some 25 or 30 years, shows no relation between aid . . . and economic development."

In their dealings with the Third World, both conservatives and liberals are reflecting their traditional values. In their overriding concern for the national security of the United States, the conservatives are upholding a centuries-old maxim that the first responsibility of a sovereign nation is its own defense. In their tendency to support existing governments, however flawed, against the forces of revolution, they are reflecting the old consevative preference for the status quo, and for the established order against the power of the mob.

For their part, in their sympathy for Third World revolutionary movements, when those movements oppose repressive regimes, the liberals are reflecting the traditional liberal sympathy for oppressed peoples. In their willingness to believe that such revolutions can succeed without turning communist or becoming agents of the Soviets, they are reflecting the traditional liberal optimism about humanity—just as the conservatives are reflecting the traditional conservative pessimism when they believe the opposite.

6

REACHING
A CONCLUSION

In a country as traditionally liberal as the United States, the distinction between being a liberal and being a conservative isn't always clear. Conserving a tradition of liberalism is, in different ways, both a liberal and a conservative thing to do.

As we've seen, the liberal experiment of Lyndon Johnson and the conservative experiment of Ronald Reagan were oddly similar in a number of ways. Each of them set for themselves an enormous goal: Johnson to wipe out poverty in America, and Reagan to reverse the whole direction in which American society had been moving for several decades. Each of them attempted to combine a large military buildup (Johnson of conventional forces, Reagan primarily of nuclear forces) with a tax cut. Each of them came under growing criticism from their own ideological camp—Johnson from the liberals, and Reagan from the conservatives. And each of them (in Reagan's case, of course, so far) came far short of achieving the ambitious goals they'd set.

Conservatives like to criticize liberals for being too eager to spend the public's money and to "mortgage the future" with large budget deficits. And yet, under the most conservative president in over fifty years, budget deficits have soared.

Liberals like to criticize conservatives for being too "tame" and "timid," and afraid to experiment. And yet, Reagan's program was referred to, even by one of its leading supporters in the Senate, as a "riverboat gamble," and his sweeping program of cutbacks in government agencies and drastic reform of the regulatory system constitutes the most daring social experiment since the New Deal.

Conservatives and liberals share many fundamental values and beliefs—beliefs in liberty, private property, the Constitution, and the future of America, among others. They've even traded positions over the years on such specific political issues as states' rights and tariffs on foreign trade.

Most Americans are not doctrinaire—meaning that they do not follow any ideological "party line," whether liberal or conservative. Most conservatives in Congress will, for one reason or another, occasionally vote on what might be considered the liberal side of a given issue. Most liberals will occasionally vote on what would be considered the conservative side. Few members of either the House or Senate are rated one hundred percent on their voting records by organizations which keep track of liberal or conservative votes on issues.

And yet, there are real and substantial differences between the two groups—both in their view of the role of America in the world, and their view of the role of the government in the lives of Americans. It's useful and important, not only to distinguish between those views, but to determine which is more compatible with your own.

In determining where you stand in this ongoing debate, so central to American political life, you might ask yourself the following questions:

Do you believe that the government takes too much money out of the hands of the productive, employed middle class in order to give it to the unproductive poor?

Do you believe that the courts are too lenient toward criminals?

Do you believe that the United States should give military assistance to Third World countries threatened by communist revolution, even if the governments of those countries are dictatorial themselves?

Do you believe that it should be up to individuals to

provide for their own health care, whether through direct payment of their own hospital and doctor bills, or by obtaining a suitable health insurance policy from a private insurance company?

Do you believe that the United States is significantly behind the Soviet Union in nuclear weaponry and has to catch up before there can be meaningful negotiations toward nuclear disarmament?

Do you believe that there is too much regulation of American industry by the government, and that the consumer and the public at large would be better off if the government would leave business decisions to the businesspeople?

Do you believe that the books in high school libraries ought to be screened to make sure that none of them promote communism?

Do you believe that it would be wrong, in a time of war, for an American to publicly criticize the country's participation in that war?

If you answered yes to most of those questions, your political views tend to be conservative.

Now consider these:

Do you believe that during hard economic times, tax money should be used to provide jobs for the unemployed?

Do you believe that the United States should refuse to give military assistance to foreign governments, such as that of South Africa, which refuse to grant basic civil rights to their own citizens?

Do you believe that the government should do more to help black Americans, Hispanic Americans, and other minorities to achieve true economic and social equality in the United States?

Do you believe that too much tax money is spent on the military?

Do you believe that the busing of both white and black children to achieve racial segregation in the schools has helped children get a better education than they would have without it?

Do you believe that the federal government should force major American corporations to employ significant numbers of black people, Hispanics, women, and members of other previously underemployed groups?

Do you believe that the government ought to prevent industries from polluting the air and water, even if that means that the industries would be less profitable?

Do you believe that the United States should work toward a mutual and verifiable nuclear freeze with the Soviet Union now, before new generations of nuclear weapons can be built by either side?

If you answered yes to most of these questions, your political views tend to be liberal.

Few Americans would answer a firm "yes" to all the questions on one of these lists, and a firm "no" to all the questions on the other. As was said in the introduction to this book, everyone is both liberal and conservative, to some extent, both in their temperament and in their political opinions. And yet, the differences between the liberal and conservative analyses of the world and of the function of government are enormous. To summarize those main lines of modern liberal and conservative thought a final time:

Liberals believe the government must play a major role in improving the lives of the nation's citizens. It should help to direct the national economy in several ways. It should provide a wide variety of programs to assist the poor, the unemployed, and the otherwise disadvantaged members of society. It should regulate business, not only to protect consumers from unscrupulous and unfair business practices and to protect the physical environment from damage, but also to promote a healthy economic environment for all. Liberals believe in the aims and many of the programs of the New Deal and of Johnson's Great Society.

To the extent that any of those programs have failed to

meet those aims, they believe that they should not simply be abolished, but rather that they should be replaced with better and, if necessary, even larger programs that can meet those aims.

Conservatives, on the other hand, are extremely doubtful about any governmental interference in the private economic affairs of citizens. While they agree that what Reagan has called a "safety net" of social programs to help the desperately poor or helpless may be needed, they believe that, in general, welfare programs only make things worse in the long run. They believe that only such traditional values as hard work, enterprise, ambition and self-reliance will ever free the poor from the grip of poverty, and that what they call "government handouts" only promote laziness and dependence.

The economic well-being of society as a whole, they say, will be achieved only through the free forces of competition in the marketplace, and therefore the best thing the government can do to promote the health of the economic environment is to stay out of the economic affairs of the citizenry as much as possible, starting by reducing both taxes and government regulation of business.

On the international front, conservatives see the world as a battleground between the west, led by the United States, and the communist world, led by the Soviet Union. The battle, they believe, must ultimately be won. Either the communists must be forced to change their beliefs, or the west must fight them. And, if we are to fight, we must be prepared to win. Consequently, the conservatives, who believe in reducing government expenditures for virtually everything else, believe in drastically increasing expenditures for the military.

Liberals, on the other hand, see the conservatives' view of the world as too apocalyptic, and consequently dangerous. In a world of nuclear overkill, they believe, such an ideologically belligerent stance could be suicidal. While it is necessary to be strong enough to deter the Soviets from ever attacking us, they feel, the only sane course is to work toward eventual peaceful relations with the Soviets. Ultimately, they believe that the American way of freedom, being superior, will be recognized as superior, even by many people around the world who now consider themselves communists.

However much the line between liberalism and conservatism may sometimes blur, however flexible individual liberals and conservatives may be, holding a liberal opinion on one issue and a conservative opinion on another, the essential differences in analysis and world view between them are vital.

Those differences dictate different courses of action—courses of action that will affect both the quality of life for Americans and the future of the human race on this planet. While liberals and conservatives differ strongly about which course of action is best for us to follow, they agree that whether America pursues a liberal course or a conservative one may well determine whether the American economy will thrive or falter, and whether the future will see war or peace.

FOR FURTHER READING

Although there are very few books designed to compare liberalism and conservatism in an objective fashion, there are many books that deal with various aspects of the two political traditions, both in the development of Western thought and in the history of American politics. They range from the long to the short, and from the concise to the complex.

For a wide-ranging examination of the two traditions, there is George Catlin's *The Story of the Political Philosophers* (New York: Whittlesy House, 1939). A long book, it introduces the reader to many of world history's most important political thinkers from ancient times to the eve of World War II. They include such notable liberal and conservative philosophers as Hobbes, Locke, and Rousseau (all of them dealt with more extensively than there has been room for here), as well as such notable figures from elsewhere on the political spectrum as Plato, Trotsky, and Hitler.

For a lengthy and interesting (although academic) study of liberalism, there's the two-volume *Human Nature and History: A Study of the Development of Liberal Political Thought,* by Robert D. Cumming (Chicago: the University of Chicago Press, 1969). A less lengthy (but still academic) study of conservative thought is Russell Amos Kirk's *The Conservative Mind, From Burke to Santayana* (Chicago: Henry Regnery, 1953), while the conservative tradition in this country is explored in Clinton Rossiter's *Conservatism in America* (New York: Alfred A. Knopf, 1962).

The liberal experiment of the New Deal is sympathetically explored from just about every angle in Arthur M. Schlesinger, Jr.'s three-volume *The Age of Roosevelt* (Boston: Houghton-Mifflin, 1956–1960); while *Why Reagan Won*, by F. Clinton White and William J. Gill, offers a sympathetic narrative history of the conservative movement in America from the defeat of Barry Goldwater to the victory of Ronald Reagan. *Thunder on the Right*, by Alan Crawford (New York: Pantheon Books, 1980), which is subtitled *The "New Right" and the Politics of Resentment*, is an interesting attack on what the author believes to be the extremists of the New Right by a journalist who is a conservative himself.

There are many programs for the future, both liberal and conservative—almost as many as there are liberal and conservative politicians. William E. Simon's *A Time for Truth* (New York: Readers Digest Press, 1978) is regarded by many American conservatives as a kind of conservative manifesto for the 1980s, while Paul Tsongas' *The Road From Here: Liberalism and Reality in the 1980s* (New York: Alfred A. Knopf, 1981) is one liberal politican's program for meeting the challenge of the nation's apparent swing to the right. A different point of view entirely is presented by Peter Clecak in his *Crooked Path: Reflections on Socialism, Conservatism and the Welfare State* (New York: Harper & Row, 1977) in which he puts forward an interesting blend of liberal and conservative principles as the best means of dealing with the realities of the modern world.

INDEX

Adams, John, 43, 74
Allied countries, U.S.
  relations with, 83–85
American political and
  social theory, 16–17,
  40–56, 58–72, 74–92,
  94–99
American Revolution,
  16–17, 40–46
Aquinas, Thomas, 9
Arms control, 68, 88–89,
  96, 97, 98–99

Bill of Rights, 46
British political and social
  theory, 9, 12–16, 29–35,
  47–49
Buckley, William F., Jr.,
  77
Burke, Edmund, 29–35, 36
Bush, Vice President
  George, 70

Carter, President Jimmy,
  66
Civil rights movement,
  U.S., 63, 80, 96
Conservatism in America
  (Rossiter), 76
Conservative aims and
  beliefs, 1–2, 29–37, 42–
  46, 51–53, 74–79, 94–
  99

domestic policy posi-
  tions, 47–56, 61–66,
  69–72, 79–83, 94–98
foreign policy posi-
  tions, 64–66, 68–69,
  79, 83–92, 95
Conservative program,
  Reagan administration's,
  66–72, 94
Considerations on France
  (de Maistre), 35
Constitution of the U.S., 26,
  42–46, 58, 74, 75, 76–77
Coolidge, President Cal-
  vin, 49–50

d'Alembert, Jean, 20
Decatur, Stephen, 75
Declaration of Indepen-
  dence, 26, 40–42
Declaration of the Rights
  of Man, 24–27, 40
de Maistre, Joseph, 35–37
Democracy, beginnings
  of, 15–17. *See also* American political and social
  theory
Descartes, René, 9–11
Diderot, Denis, 20
Domestic policy, liberal
  and conservative posi-
  tions on, 47–56, 61–66,
  69–72, 79–83, 94–98

102

British, 9, 12–16, 29–35, 47–49

French, 9–11, 16–17, 20, 21–22, 24–27, 29, 35–37

radical, 77–79

Property rights, 33–34, 74, 75–76

Radical political theory, 77–79

Reagan, President Ronald, 50, 66–72, 77, 94

Reflections on the Revolution in France (Burke), 34–35

Reign of Terror, 27–29

Religious faith and political authority, 4–5, 8, 32, 36–37

Rights of the individual, 40, 51–53, 54, 78–79, 80–83, 96. *See also* Social contract

Robespierre, Maximilien, 21–22, 28, 29

Roosevelt, President Franklin D., 55, 58, 61

Roosevelt, President Theodore, 50

Rossiter, Clinton, 76

Rousseau, Jean Jacques, 21, 24, 33

Saint-Just, Louis, 28, 29

Schurz, Carl, 75

Slavery, abolition of, 26, 53–54

Smith, Adam, 47–49

Social contract, theory of the, 11–16, 33

Social issues policies, 62–63, 68, 69, 79–83, 95–96, 97, 98

States' rights policies, 47, 50–51, 79

Third world countries, U.S. relations with, 87, 89–92, 95, 96

U.S.S.R., U.S. relations with, 68, 85–89, 96, 97, 98–99

U.S. foreign relations allied countries, 83–85 third world countries, 87, 89–92, 95, 96 U.S.S.R., 68, 85–89

U.S. News and World Report, 71

Vietnam conflict, 64–66

Voltaire, Francois Marie Arouet de, 20

War on Poverty, Johnson's 61–66, 94

Washington, President George, 83

Wealth of Nations (Smith), 47–49